The
Complete Jogger

The Complete Jogger
Bruce Tulloh

Medical contributor Dr J. Davies

M

Line drawings by Joan Thompson
Picture research by Juliet Brightmore
The publishers wish to thank Weidenfeld and Nicolson Ltd
for their kind permission to reproduce '100 steps to superfitness'
from *Naturally Fit*, Bruce Tulloh, 1976

Imperial measurements have been used throughout the work:
a conversion table is included in the Appendices

First published 1979 simultaneously by
Macmillan London Ltd
London and Basingstoke
(Associated companies in Delhi, Dublin,
Hong Kong, Johannesburg, Lagos, Melbourne,
New York, Singapore and Tokyo)
and Pan Books Ltd

Printed and bound by
Redwood Burn Ltd, Trowbridge and Esher

British Library Cataloguing in Publication Data
Tulloh, Bruce
  The Complete Jogger
  I . Jogging
  1. Title
  613.7'1   GV494
ISBN 0 333 25718 9

Contents

The complete jogger

1 Twenty-one reasons why you should jog

Because it is what the human body is designed to do

As Robert Ardrey pointed out, humans are distinguished from apes more by their buttocks than their brains. Of all the primates, *Homo sapiens* was the only one to come down from the trees and walk upright on two feet. The change to a hunting way of life, with a mixed diet rather than a purely vegetable diet, took place over two million years ago. Since then humans have relied on their ability to hunt or gather food. The fact that humans have lost their fur, according to Desmond Morris, is thought to be due to the need for our ancestors to run long distances in catching their prey. In the hot climates in which we evolved, a hairy animal would overheat during a long chase. We did not become good sprinters, like the cheetah, but we developed the hands for grasping weapons, the brains for organizing the hunt and the legs and lungs of long-distance runners. If you doubt me, look at a gorilla or a chimpanzee at the zoo. They are designed for hanging around and eating bananas. You are designed to run.

Because it will help control your weight

Jogging will help to reduce your weight in four ways. Firstly, you will lose weight by sweating – but this is only a short-term loss, since the water and salts will be replaced when you drink.

Secondly, you will burn up extra calories by taking extra exercise. The amount you lose will depend on whether you eat more. If you eat a lot of extra food you will not lose anything at all – even marathon runners eventually reach a fixed weight once they are eating enough to make up for all the miles they run. However, for the ordinary person, jogging does not in fact cause an increase in appetite; if anything, it slightly reduces it, because you will not feel comfortable running on a full stomach, and after you've jogged you will be inclined to drink something rather than eat a lot.

Thirdly, running will speed up your metabolism (the rate at which you burn up food) at rest.

Fourthly, running will make you hot and (if you do it regularly) your body will react as it would if you were living in a hot climate, gradually cutting down any fat stored.

All these effects add up: the amount of fat loss – a pound for every 15 or 20 miles run – may not sound very much, but on my schedules that means a stone in six months.

Because it will make your heart stronger

The heart is made of muscle, and like any other muscle it will become stronger if it is used and weaker if it is not used. A sudden increase in the rate at which it has to work is bad for it, but a gradual increase trains your heart so that it acquires a greater working capacity – like that of an athlete. The average person's pulse rate at rest is 70 to 80 beats a minute; mine is 48 beats a minute. This means that my heart is working very easily at rest, and when I have to do something strenuous it very rarely has to work at peak rate. If my heart rate doubles, it is still below 100, and it can go up to 180 quite happily. When the heart rate of the unfit person doubles, it will be up to about 150 to 160 beats a minute, which is getting pretty close to the safety margin. The heart of the trained runner is stronger and more versatile than that of the untrained person, and so it is less at risk.

Because it will improve your circulation

Most importantly, running improves the flow of blood through your coronary artery and its branches. Within the heart muscle itself, extra capillary vessels develop. The major blood vessels also become stronger and able to deal comfortably with greater work-rates. In your working muscles the capillary blood vessels will increase too, giving you better circulation through your limbs. This means that the cells get a better supply of oxygen and food, and waste products are taken away more quickly.

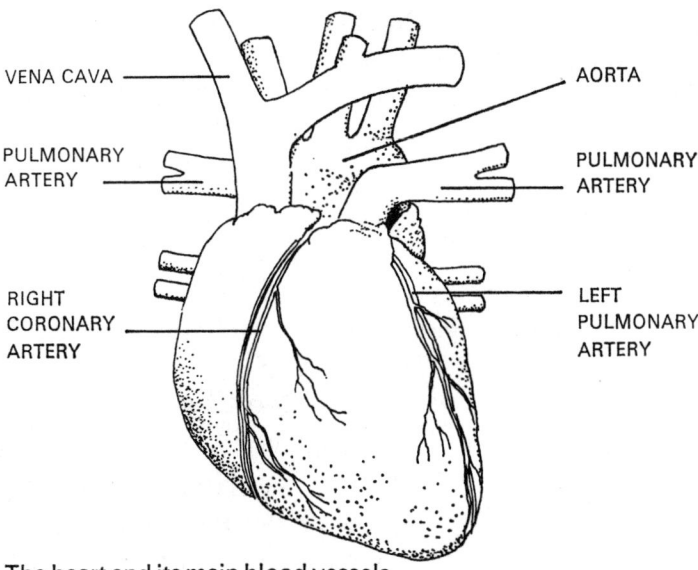

VENA CAVA

PULMONARY ARTERY

RIGHT CORONARY ARTERY

AORTA

PULMONARY ARTERY

LEFT PULMONARY ARTERY

The heart and its main blood vessels

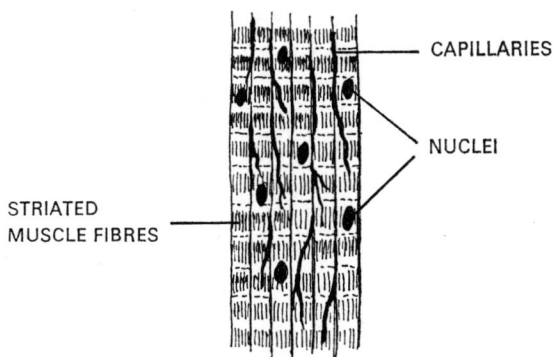

CAPILLARIES

NUCLEI

STRIATED MUSCLE FIBRES

Capillary blood supply in leg muscle

Because it will decrease the amount of fat in your bloodstream

Extensive research has been done in Great Britain by the Medical Research Council. The Council has found that during a three-month exercise programme subjects reduced the amount of cholesterol and other fatty substances in their blood. It is these lipids which often lead to 'clogging' of the arteries and therefore to high blood pressure and increased risk of heart failure. It has been known for years that young women suffer far less than men from heart attacks, and this appears to be closely linked to the presence in their blood of a certain type of lipo-protein. Very recently, it has been found that runners actually change their body chemistry, converting their lipo-protein into the safer 'female' type. As a result harmful lipids are much less likely to build up in the circulatory system.

Because it will normalize your blood pressure

In the tests referred to, it was found that over a three-month period of training the subjects' blood pressure decreased significantly. Their resting pulse rates also declined, showing that their hearts were not having to work so hard. One of the reasons for this is that the proportion of fat in the body is decreased. Fatty tissues offer resistance to the circulating blood. It has been said that a pound of fat adds a mile of capillary resistance and, unlike the capillaries in the working muscles which are opened up only when they are needed, the heart has continually to force blood through these fatty tissues. High blood pressure, as we know, is the main indication of suscepti-bility to heart attacks, strokes or kidney complaints.

In the case of someone suffering from low blood pressure, the effects of exercise are to strengthen the heart and raise the metabolic rate. This brings blood pressure closer to normal values.

Because it will diminish the damaging effects of stress

Most heart attacks and strokes occur in periods of great emotional stress – watching the World Cup, worrying about your business. Stress causes the release into your blood stream of the hormone adrenalin. This in turn causes your heart rate and blood pressure to rise, besides causing an increase in blood viscosity and an increase in the amount of sugar in your blood. Regular running opens up the capillaries, which lowers the blood pressure, and burns up the sugar. Your heart and blood vessels being stronger than normal, will be better able to stand the increased rate, and the chances of irregularities arising in your heart beat are decreased.

Because it will lessen your chances of having a heart attack

In addition to the factors mentioned above, the blood vessels of the trained person have fewer fatty deposits. The chances of thrombosis are therefore reduced. If a branch of the coronary artery *did* become blocked, the effects on a trained person would be less damaging, because his coronary artery is more richly branched, and the heart is less likely to run out of oxygen and stop working.

Because it will lessen your chances of a stroke

Strokes are caused by a failure of the oxygen supply to the brain following a cerebral haemorrhage. If your heart is working normally, the surges of pressure which cause the haemorrhage are less likely. The effects of exercise will also give you a more robust cerebral vascular system – the same effect as the yoga practioner gets from standing on his head.

Because you will visit your doctor less often

The only times I see my doctor are when we are both out jogging or we are having a drink. He and his wife run regularly and are very good advertisements for what they preach. In the past ten years since I stopped competing internationally I have never had to miss a day's work, or a day's training, through illness. The only blot on the ten years before that was an attack of measles. This could be luck, but I doubt it.

Although being healthy is not the same thing as being fit, by looking after your fitness you are also taking care of your health. Most of the minor troubles which send people off to their doctors – things like headaches, insomnia, indigestion, constipation, anxiety and depression, simply do not trouble the runner. You may still pick up infections, but if you have a good routine of eating, sleeping and exercise, you will have a greater resistance to them. You may get some of the runner's problems in the first few weeks, but you will soon learn how to avoid them.

Because it will increase your life expectancy

To justify this claim I could simply point to the factor of weight loss. If you are ten per cent overweight your life expectancy is reduced by 13 per cent. In people 45 per cent overweight life expectancy is reduced by 50 per cent. The chances of developing diabetes, having a heart attack, a stroke or kidney trouble all go up enormously with increased weight.

Life expectancy studies carried out on groups of active and inactive people show that death occurs earlier in the less active people. The biggest killers are cardiovascular diseases, which affect active people far less often. In a recent American study, the best indicator of life expectancy in males was the amount of exercise they were taking in their forties.

Because you will feel better after it

The greatest argument for running is the feeling of mental and physical well-being you get after a good session. The first few sessions may be a bit of a struggle, but when your body has got used to the new regime, which will take about two weeks, you will start to feel the difference. If you haven't been used to exercise for a few years you will be surprised how good you feel – it is a feeling of youth. It is not merely that you move in an easy, relaxed manner, with muscles that do what you want them to do: you also experience a delightful feeling of calm and satisfaction.

Because you will look better

The first effects will be that you tone up your muscles, making your body firmer and better looking even before you start to lose weight. The second thing is that you slim down your legs – this will show after three or four weeks – and then you will gradually start to lose fat from the rest of your body. The fresh air and improved circulation will make your skin look better, and you will get a light tan as well as a glow of health. It will take months to make a lot of difference to your weight, but all the time you will have the morale booster of knowing that the more you jog, the better you look.

Because you will become more self-confident

In the jogging programmes (Chapters 4, 5 and 6) you start from the possible and go on to achieve the impossible – or what was impossible for you when you started. After a few weeks you will find yourself able to do things which you did not think you were capable of and, what is more, you will have a record of what you have already done, and the progress you have made. This self-improvement will carry over into your daily life. Once you have found that you can extend your limits in one direction, you will find that you can develop in other ways. All things become possible; you become the controller of your own fate, a free agent.

The training you do is a form of stress. You will adapt to it, learn how to handle it, and then increase it. The stresses of ordinary life will begin to seem less important. You will stop being afraid of difficult situations because you will be used to going through the stress and coming safely out the other end. You will know that you can recover quickly from tiredness, and will not be afraid of pushing yourself hard when the need arises. You will know that you can do something that most other people cannot do, and so you will become less afraid of competing with others.

Because you will learn about yourself

We all have images of ourselves. By attempting to follow the training programme you will put your personality and willpower to the test. How you make out will give you a more realistic knowledge of yourself. You will find that there are times when you take on more than you can handle, and you are forced to quit. That will make you more humble, and more understanding of the failures of others. You will find that you can sometimes overcome both your tiredness and your fear of pain. This will give you a better knowledge of your full potential. The solid achievement of having carried through a training programme will give you confidence in your ability to see things through. In Kipling's words, 'If you can meet with triumph and disaster, and treat those two impostors just the same' you will have a better understanding of where reality lies.

Because you will suffer less from depression

Whatever the hormonal or psychological reasons may be, the majority of trained runners are positive, forward-looking people, who are not easily put down by trivial things. Maybe it is just that they are worrying so much about their running that they have no time to worry about anything else!

Because you will lead a fuller life

The fitness programmes are designed to make you a stronger, more capable, more energetic person. Even though you may be spending two or three hours a week running or preparing to run, you will find that you can fit more into your life, not less. The feeling of physical.well-being puts you into the frame of mind where you want to get more out of life. You will enjoy your food and drink more. You will be more perceptive, because increased fitness will sharpen your senses. Because you have been raising your own standards, you will expect more out of life, and so you will get more out of life.

Because you will be at the forefront of a growing movement

It may not be a very noble reason, but we all like to be admired. If you can do what other people would like to be able to do, but haven't actually achieved, then you get a lot of self-satisfaction. In fact, you will have to be careful about being too smug about it.

Because you will get to know your neighbourhood better

Once you start going out walking and jogging, you will be surprised how many new places you will discover. In order to avoid the traffic, you will go into quiet side roads and housing estates that you would not normally see. You will start looking for parks and playing fields where you can jog on the grass, and for hills where you can do a bit of different training. Within a few weeks you will know every footpath and lane in your area, and they will have a new meaning for you. They somehow belong to you, because you have experienced them. Going on foot you have time to smell the smells and hear the sounds that the man in his car misses and ignores. You have time to look at the people at work, at the girls going by, and you will notice trees, flowers in window boxes, dogs and babies. After a while they will come to know you. You will get a friendly nod from postmen, roadsweepers, shopkeepers. You will become a part of the scene.

Because you will meet new people

I have run in most parts of the world – in the streets of Moscow, New York, Hong Kong, Auckland, Nairobi, Los Angeles, Rome, Budapest, Helsinki, Perth, Paris and Stockholm, as well as innumerable beaches, tracks, woods and hilltops.

In most places I have come across fellow joggers. They may be serious athletes, or middle-aged men jogging for their health. Sometimes I've exchanged a few words, more often we've just nodded and smiled. As soon as you see another runner you have seen another friend – even though he may be a rival as well. All those who run have that common experience. It is like sharing a collective unconscious. We all go through the same difficulties. We all share the same dream.

Nowhere will you find greater camaraderie than among long-distance runners. If you go to any of the big road races – like the São Paulo, the Boston, the old Nos Galan, you find people giving each other lifts, beds, friendly advice, linament, glucose tablets, and beer. Even if you are just a humble, round-the-block jogger, you are part of that world.

Because deep down you know you are doing the right thing

This comes back to what I said right at the beginning. It's not just that you know scientifically that it's good for you, or because you are exciting the envy and admiration of your neighbours. The more you run, the more you know that it is right to run. It becomes like the mantra or the prayer-wheel, a means of working out your own salvation. Every run that you finish represents a new experience, as precious as a little piece of eternity captured and stored away.

2 Jogging for women

Can women do anything men can do?

In running, a woman who has really trained well can beat 99 per cent of the untrained men in her age group. The differences between top-class male and female performances are narrowing continually. Women have run 400 metres in under 49 seconds, 800 metres ($\frac{1}{2}$ mile) in under 1 minute 55 seconds and 1500 metres in 3 minutes 55 seconds. In the longer distances the women's 10,000-metres ($6\frac{1}{4}$-miles) record is approaching 30 minutes. Compare this with the times expected over 4 and 5 miles for joggers. In the marathon the women's record is now down to 2 hours 35 minutes as against 2 hours 8 minutes for men, but I expect women to break 2 hours 30 minutes by 1980.

On average women have slightly less strong muscles and a slightly lower oxygen intake than men for their body weight. This means that they are not quite as fast: an international level woman is about on a par with a good schoolboy athlete. On the other hand their powers of endurance are just as great, their food reserves, in the form of fat, are greater, their flexibility is greater, they have fewer heart attacks than men and they live longer. Since the differences in running ability between the sexes is so slight, women are able to jog as easily as men.

Do women need to jog?

Many women are turned off by the idea of physical exercise and produce arguments to give themselves excuses such as 'I can look after my weight by dieting.' This may be true, but is it, in fact, working? Someone who is cutting down on their food may be lacking in energy as well as missing some essential foodstuffs, whereas the woman who is jogging as well as watching her diet will actually be gaining in muscular strength and will have more vitality.

'I get all the exercise I need in housework.' Women often spend many hours a day on their feet doing housework and shopping. Unfortunately, this does nothing at all to strengthen your heart and you are not burning up the calories very fast either. Housework simply does not make your heart work fast enough.

'With children to look after, I just haven't got the time.' If your children are five years old or more, you can take them jogging with you – they will enjoy it if you make a game of it. If they are toddlers, or totally pram-bound, you can still take them to the park or the beach. If you cannot get anyone to keep an eye on them for 10 minutes you can jog in circles round them. Even if you are never more than 50 yards away, you will have a lap of over 300 yards, just over 5 of which makes a mile. In a fun-run recently I saw a couple pushing their toddler along the pavement in his pushchair as they jogged, and they did 5 miles!

'I feel shy of going out jogging by myself.' Men are just as bad in this respect, but I have made some suggestions on page 87 for overcoming this problem.

How does jogging affect your looks?

The healthier you are, the more attractive you look. Look at people who come back from skiing. Look at all the model-girls and film-stars who jog. Look at how much exercise ballet-dancers and chorus-girls take – five or six hours a day – without it spoiling their looks.

Healthy does not have to mean weather-beaten. Generally, fresh, moist air is very good for the complexion, but if the weather is very cold or very dry you can always protect your face with cream and your hair with a scarf.

Does jogging have any special advantages for women?

The advantages listed for men apply equally to women. It is a particularly good activity if you are house-bound because you can start and finish at your own front door – you don't need to take the car anywhere, or to make a booking for a court. Since women can jog as well as or better than many men, it is good for the ego. The charts given in later chapters make no distinction between the sexes – only between degrees of fitness and age.

Like all sports, jogging has the advantage of helping you to make friends and meet people in a new neighbourhood, and unlike most sports it requires no skill and little expense.

Can you jog while pregnant?

Yes, you can. In Sweden, where orienteering is a major sport for women, they go on competing in races until they are up to six months pregnant, and are competing again when the baby is three months old. So jogging, which is a much gentler form of running, is quite acceptable until you are six months pregnant. After that, the extra weight will make running very uncomfortable, and I would recommend you to carry on with regular walking, which can be done until the child is born.

How soon after childbirth can you start jogging again?

Obviously you will talk to your doctor about this, but you should be able to start again six weeks after the birth. If you have been walking as much as possible it will not take you long to get back to full fitness. The six-week beginner's programme in Chapter 4 would be a suitable post-natal one.

How much does menstruation affect jogging?

Very little. Women athletes find that their performance is a little below par during and just before menstruation, but that is at high speed, where they are running, say 2 miles in under

10 minutes. Menstruation is a time to take the training a little bit easier – do a long slow session rather than a time trial, and use two of the week's rest days if you need them.

Because of the loss of blood during menstruation, women are affected more by anaemia than men. If you are anaemic, it will affect your running performance because you have fewer red corpuscles, less haemoglobin, and so can take up less oxygen. Consult your doctor if you are feeling below par and have a haemoglobin check. Your doctor will probably prescribe additional iron in your diet.

Jogging shoes for women

If you are used to wearing high heels most of the time, your feet will be slightly distorted and your toes may be cramped. When you put on running shoes it may take a bit of time for you to get used to the different way your weight is distributed. Read over the section 'How to Jog' in the next chapter. You might need some flexibility exercises for your ankles as well, because they will be put at a different angle when you are jogging. Do *not* try to run on tip-toe – start off running on your heels and the flat of your foot, so that your weight is evenly distributed. You need to take particular care to get a pair of shoes that fit you properly.

3 Getting started in jogging

Jogging is safe but . . .

It is bad to see a headline 'Man dies while jogging' but it is much worse for the man. In fact more people die lying in bed or watching TV than jogging, but we must still take every possible precaution.

Of the thousands of people who read these lines, it is probable that several hundred of them have some undisclosed abnormality of their cardiovascular system. In most of those cases a graduated exercise programme, started gently, will improve their condition, but there will be a few who have not taken exercise for a long time and who have a heart condition which would be seriously aggravated by rushing out to jog.

Even these people can be helped by running. Dr Kavanagh, in Toronto, runs a cardiac rehabilitation group and the patients

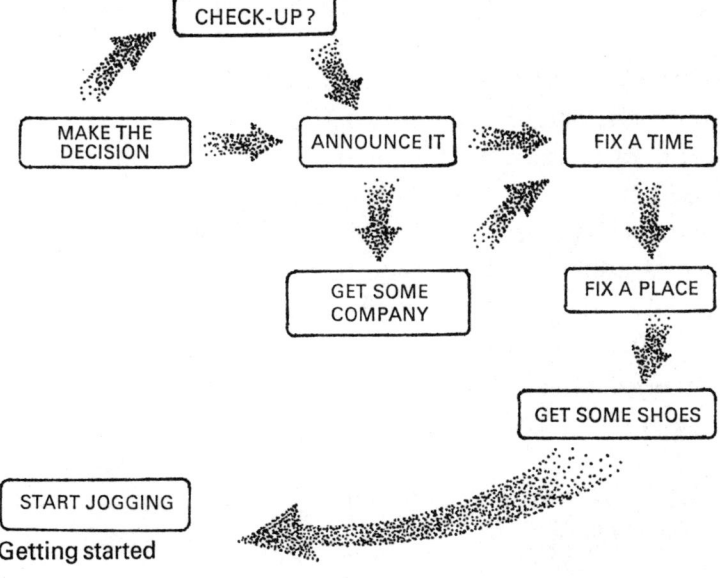

Getting started

regularly go running. Dr Kavanagh entered seven of them, all of whom had had serious heart attacks before coming under his care, in the Boston marathon, and all of them completed the course – because they had the proper training, with medical supervision.

Jogging is considerably less dangerous than most sports, except perhaps ping-pong! It is, or should be, non-competitive, there is no physical contact, there are no bats or balls to injure you, you can't fall off and you can't drown. Most important of all, the level of exercise is controlled by you, the jogger, and if it gets too hard you can always slow down or stop. That said, there are some cases in which it is advisable to have a check-up before starting.

Who needs a check-up?

Anyone who has had a serious illness in the last year.
Anyone who has a family history of heart trouble.
Anyone who is seriously overweight (more than 15 pounds over on the weight chart).
Anyone who is over 35 and who has not taken strenuous exercise within the last two years.
Anyone who feels chest pains or acute breathlessness after breaking into a run.

What sort of check-up is necessary?

See your own doctor and explain why you think you need a check-up. As he knows your medical history, he may be able to advise you on how gently to start, in which case you can go on to Chapter 3. He will probably check your heart rate and blood pressure. If both of these are high, he will probably want to give you an electro-cardiogram (ECG) test. This will show up any abnormalities in your heart-beat. To be certain, you should have an ECG done while you are actually doing exercise, either jogging on the spot, riding a static bicycle or stepping on and off a bench. This is the only real safe test, as some abnormalities may not show up unless you are under physical stress.

Weight chart : men

Height		Small frame				Medium frame				Large frame			
ft	in	st	lb	st	lb	st	lb	st	lb	st	lb	st	lb
5	1	8	0 –	8	8	8	6 –	9	3	9	1 –	10	1
5	2	8	3 –	8	12	8	9 –	9	7	9	3 –	10	4
5	3	8	6 –	9	0	8	12 –	9	10	9	6 –	10	8
5	4	8	8 –	9	3	9	1 –	9	13	9	9 –	10	12
5	5	8	12 –	9	7	9	4 –	10	3	9	12 –	11	2
5	6	9	2 –	9	11	9	8 –	10	7	10	2 –	11	7
5	7	9	6 –	10	1	9	12 –	10	12	10	7 –	11	12
5	8	9	10 –	10	5	10	2 –	11	2	10	11 –	12	2
5	9	10	0 –	10	10	10	6 –	11	6	11	1 –	12	6
5	10	10	4 –	11	0	10	10 –	11	11	11	5 –	12	11
5	11	10	8 –	11	4	11	0 –	12	2	11	10 –	13	2
6	0	10	12 –	11	8	11	4 –	12	7	12	0 –	13	7
6	1	11	2 –	11	13	11	8 –	12	12	12	5 –	13	12
6	2	11	6 –	12	3	11	13 –	13	3	12	10 –	14	3
6	3	11	10 –	12	7	12	4 –	13	8	13	0 –	14	8

Weight chart : women

Height		Small frame				Medium frame				Large frame			
ft	in	st	lb	st	lb	st	lb	st	lb	st	lb	st	lb
4	8	6	8 –	7	0	6	12 –	7	9	7	6 –	8	7
4	9	6	10 –	7	3	7	0 –	7	12	7	8 –	8	10
4	10	6	12 –	7	6	7	3 –	8	1	7	11 –	8	13
4	11	7	1 –	7	9	7	6 –	8	4	8	0 –	9	2
5	0	7	4 –	7	12	7	9 –	8	7	8	3 –	9	5
5	1	7	7 –	8	1	7	12 –	8	10	8	6 –	9	8
5	2	7	10 –	8	4	8	1 –	9	0	8	9 –	9	12
5	3	7	13 –	8	7	8	4 –	9	4	8	13 –	10	2
5	4	8	2 –	8	11	8	8 –	9	9	9	3 –	10	6
5	5	8	6 –	9	1	8	12 –	9	13	9	7 –	10	10
5	6	8	10 –	9	5	9	2 –	10	3	9	11 –	11	0
5	7	9	0 –	9	9	9	6 –	10	7	10	1 –	11	4
5	8	9	4 –	10	0	9	10 –	10	11	10	5 –	11	9
5	9	9	8 –	10	4	10	0 –	11	9	10	9 –	12	0
5	10	9	12 –	10	8	10	4 –	11	5	10	13 –	12	5

Places to jog

If you are determined or crazy enough, you can jog anywhere, but unless the environment is right you probably won't manage to keep your programme going. The secret is to make it as easy and pleasant for yourself as possible. The best places are the ones nearest to home. It is better to use something on your doorstep which is satisfactory, than to insist on going somewhere that is perfect but further away.

The most important thing is that you should be able to run in a free and relaxed fashion. That means finding a place where there are no crowds, heavy traffic, prams, mad dogs, blind corners and ditches. The size of the area is important – if it is too small you will get bored with going round and round, and if it is too big the size of the circuit may be so daunting that you only go out when you are feeling really good. The ideal size of circuit for the beginner is between half a mile and $1\frac{1}{2}$ miles.

The type of surface is less important (see Chapter 6) than the location, but ideally it should be shortish grass, and either flat or undulating. In Great Britain the nicest places are village cricket pitches – round the boundary and *behind* the sight screen – school playing fields and urban parks. If you are not near a nice patch of grass (which is unlikely because schools and cricket pitches are found everywhere), then I suggest you look for a nice quiet housing estate. Many of them are arranged on a circular pattern, and there is often a strip of grass between the houses and the road. The advantage of this is that it will have lighted street lamps in the winter. If you run on the road rather than the grass the running surface will always be the same, so it is easy to compare times.

After that, and in no particular order, good places to jog are: tow-paths, riverside walks, quiet side-roads, marked footpaths, beaches, moorland, Forestry Commission firebreaks, round the edge of fields after harvest time, and university precincts.

Places where it is *possible* for the determined person to jog are railway platforms, airport buildings, up the stairs of office blocks, round flat roof-tops, through the streets of any city, the upper decks of large ships, the corridors of large hotels and round the Red Square in Moscow.

Footpaths in Alpine countries and ski-trails in Scandinavia, Canada and the USA are ideal. These are often indicated by arrows printed on the trees, and the length of the trail is sometimes also given.

Places not to jog

It is stupid to go jogging in a place where the chances of doing yourself an injury outweigh the chances of doing yourself some good. In this category I put places where the ground is so uneven or covered in vegetation that you are likely to fall or twist an ankle, such as freshly ploughed land, stony beaches, or deep heather.

Harm may also result from a polluted atmosphere or thick fog, but the chief troubles are due to what I call social reasons. Humans are very conscious of their proprietorial rights and a strange figure running on their land can be seen as a threat. Don't go running close to military establishments in Zambia or Iran, or anywhere where the police have itchy trigger fingers. Don't go running on tracks that lead into small villages in out-of-the-way places; you will upset the villagers and have all the dogs in the place after you. Don't run across fields which have crops growing or animals in them. Don't run in school playing fields until you have made some effort to get permission, and don't run on the grass in European countries unless the area is actually designated as a running place. Don't run on Italian beaches – they will charge you for it. As a final piece of advice – it is worth finding out who owns the land you intend running on. If you go and ask permission you will avoid making an enemy and you may even make a friend.

The time to jog

Any time is better than no time at all, and all the rules I am about to put down may be broken.

The best times to run are just before a meal (whether lunch, dinner or even breakfast) or two hours after you have eaten. By experience you should know at which time of day you feel most alert and this is the best time to go out.

If you have had a hard day's work and a tiring journey home, the best time to go out is immediately you get in – otherwise you will probably sit down, have something to drink, and never get out at all.

It is better to run at a fixed time every day, so that less mental effort need be put into arranging it. Then you can plan your day, leaving that time available for your running. It is for this reason that so many people run before breakfast, even though it is not physically the best time of day for most of us.

If your office provides washing facilities, take the opportunity to run during your lunch-hour. You can get the changing and running done in 30 minutes, and you will save money and calories by spending less time in the pub.

It is good to run at a time when you know others will be running, because then you can arrange to join up with them.

It is a good idea to go jogging before a party – provided you have enough time to shower and change afterwards. You will arrive at the party feeling less tense, more at peace with yourself, and more awake.

The time not to jog

It is unwise to run when you are suffering from infections, such as flu, a bad cold or a cough. There have even been one or two deaths due to very hard training during influenza infections.

It is obviously not a good thing to run directly after eating, because at that time quite a lot of blood is flowing to your stomach and intestines and less is available for your working muscles.

Don't jog when you are drunk. You are liable to trip over and bump into things and apart from giving jogging a bad name you are more likely to get run over. So far as I know, no one has been charged with being drunk in charge of a pair of

1 *One of the best ways to get started is to make jogging a pastime for all the family. Note that you won't need special clothing in the early stages. (The Sports Council)*

2 *Jogging will appeal to all the family: the author with his wife Sue, son Clive (16), daughters Jo-Jo and Katherine (both 8), and dog, Oliver. (Bruce Tulloh)*

3 *Having got started find others to join you and somewhere nice for you all to run. Note the leader's shoes — more important than fancy track suits. (Topix)*

4 *Joggers using the Fitness Trail in Sefton Park, Liverpool. More expenditure on amenities such as this would soon be compensated by reduced community health costs. (Liverpool Daily Post and Echo)*

5 This group at the Burnley General Hospital in Lancashire shows that joggers come in all shapes and sizes, and that they all enjoy it. (Topix)

6 An ideal round-the-park circuit: you can use the grass or the path depending on the weather. (Topix)

7 *Jogging in the summer means shedding track suits. If you want to look as good as this start running in January!* (Camera Press)

8 *Jogging in the winter requires more dedication, as well as the right clothing. The headgear is important in conditions like these. (Sport and General)*

9 *You are never too old to start, as long as you start carefully: the over-sixty group in the* Sunday Times Fun Run. *(Topix)*

10 *Probably his doctor wouldn't recommend it, but this man's dedication shows what can be done. (Times Newspapers Ltd)*

11 *MPs Teddy Taylor and Harry Ewing out to support a 'Fit for Life' campaign. These are the kind of people — overworked and overweight — who need exercise most but rarely take it. (Sport and General)*

Adidas shoes, so don't be the first one. Running with a hangover is alright and will in fact make you feel a lot better afterwards.

When to give yourself a rest

There is nothing sacred about going out unfailingly every day. The object is to keep yourself in a state of healthy equilibrium. If you are deeply tired or feeling weak, don't go running – you will only get yourself more tired and run down. Experience alone will tell you when the tiredness is real and when it is mainly psychological.

Remember that the fitness is supposed to be adding to your enjoyment of life, not spoiling it. In the first four weeks you may need to apply willpower to keep yourself going out regularly, but then it should become a habit. Once you have got a few weeks behind you, it would be silly to waste all that effort and allow yourself to slip back. But a habit should not become an obsession. There will be times when you will really loathe the thought of going out. So don't go. Do something else which you enjoy doing. All runners experience staleness from time to time, and although it is mainly psychological it is none the less real and should not be ignored. A day off can easily be integrated into the weekly pattern, and a week off won't do any harm, set in the context of year-round activity. One of Great Britain's most successful long-distance men, Ken Norris, told me that he used to take one week off from training every three months, and one month off every year. This helped him to retain a fresh approach, and contributed to his staying in top-class competition for ten years. Mind you, I haven't gone a week without a run in 25 years, and I still thoroughly enjoy it; it really is a matter of individual taste.

Fixing the daily routine

I have already mentioned the best times to jog. You must decide what suits you best. The schedules in Chapters 5 and 6 require you to go out three or four times a week. The weekly total matters more than what you do any one day, so you can do two or three successive days, or alternate days.

Let's say you decide on three weekdays plus one run at the weekend. The next decision is the amount of time you need. We can fix that at 40 minutes, giving you time for the running and the changing either side. You must also choose at what time to run and where. If there is some regular time when a group of your friends go out, it is well worth joining them once a week, even if it is slightly inconvenient. You will get a psychological boost from talking about your progress, and even if the sport is not meant to be competitive, you will not want to be shown up! Being in a group you will give each other motivation, mutual back-patting and an opportunity to share each other's problems.

This leaves you with three other days to go out on your own, or with a member of the family. You have to be a bit selfish about this, if you want to achieve anything. You must say: 'Seven o'clock is the time I go jogging, whether anyone is coming with me or not.' I've found from experience that if the time becomes too flexible, then many beginners will drop out completely. After a few years it becomes an addiction, and you go out whatever the time or place, but in the early days you must make it easy for yourself to jog, and difficult to back out of it. Once you have decided on a time members of the family will soon start to say: 'Nearly seven o'clock, isn't it time for your jog?'

If you are following my schedules, you already have a plan of what to do during the week, so all you have to do is fix the actual route, and make sure that you have your running things ready to use when you want them. In the first weeks you will learn the routes you prefer. I suggest you vary these slightly, so that you don't cover any twice in one week. If you come to each route only once every one or two weeks, you are more likely to notice your improvement. Personal preferences come in here. Some people like to have exactly the same run to do every day of the week, so that they don't have to think about it, whereas some like the stimulation of running in different places.

If you are going to run at work, or on the way back from work, make sure that your clothing is clean and ready just when you want it. If you have washed and ironed your shorts, and put them in your briefcase or bag for the lunchtime run, you can hardly come home with them unworn at the end of the week.

In all these things – naming a time, committing yourself publicly to a certain programme, getting people to run with you – you are reinforcing your original decision, so that it becomes almost impossible to back out without losing face. You are re-designing your life pattern so that running becomes an integral part of it.

What to wear

Not having the right clothes is not a good excuse: I frequently jog across London in my ordinary business clothes. On the other hand, having the right clothing is a great asset, because it helps you to look forward to your run. If you look good you will want to be seen more often, so you will go out more often. Offering to buy your spouse a track suit is a good way to get her or him out to keep you company.

The first thing is to get a good pair of training shoes. Tennis shoes with perhaps an added foam rubber insole will do for a start, but if you are going to be running regularly, particularly if most of it is on roads, then you must have something which will give your feet proper support. The right kind of training shoes will have a 'gristle' rubber sole and a soft leather or leather-and-nylon upper.

Between sole and upper is a wedge of firm rubber, which gives a lot of padding under the heel. I would suggest getting one of the well-known makes to start off with, and then, when you know what you want, you may be able to shop around for the second pair. A good pair of training shoes should last you well over a thousand miles, which is over a year for the average jogger.

The shoes should fit firmly but not tightly when worn with

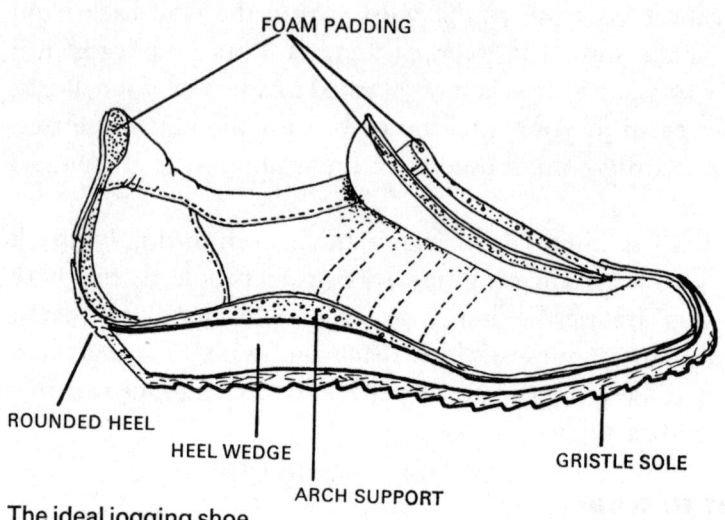

FOAM PADDING

ROUNDED HEEL

HEEL WEDGE

ARCH SUPPORT

GRISTLE SOLE

The ideal jogging shoe

a woollen or absorbent sock. If they stretch slightly with wear, you can wear an extra thin sock inside the absorbent one.

The clothing should keep your body temperature normal, as well as make you look good. You can go out in almost any conditions if you have the right clothing – I have Canadian friends who jog regularly at 20 degrees below zero. As I have said before, the human being is a warm weather animal: you must start off warm. As you jog you get warmer, due to the heat released by your muscles, so you can take off some of your clothes as the run progresses. As you get warmer you sweat, and this sweat must be allowed to evaporate. You shouldn't, therefore, wear anything too tight. During summer I go out in T-shirt and shorts, with Y-fronts underneath. If the day is slightly cool I put on a track suit, made of a cotton and nylon mixture, and keep it on for the first mile or so. If it is a chilly day I keep the track suit top on for the whole run – the legs generate plenty of heat. If it is below about 5°C (41°F) I keep the track suit on for the whole run.

It is worth having two track suits if you are going to run a lot. One should be heavier with a hooded top, When it is really wet, or when there is a strong cold wind, I wear a thin nylon anorak, hooded, over the top of my track suit and gloves.

If you are going to take running seriously, you will need two sets of shorts and T-shirts, one or two track suits, a pair of training shoes and an anorak. Even with this expense running is a cheap hobby. There is no limit to the number of miles you can cover once you have got the gear. The only problem is that you may get so slim that the track suit will become too big for you! Per hour or mile, you won't find a cheaper sport: the entire cost of the clothing, most of which will last for several years, is no more than a single servicing bill for your car.

Switching on mentally

So, you have got yourself organized, bought your kit and established a schedule of what you ought to do. The next problem to face is that you still have to take that first crucial step. This is the time when all sorts of reasons for not going out will spring to mind – bits of work to be done, people to see, papers to read. I never have this trouble, because, firstly, I love the sensation of running, and, secondly, I know that it's doing me good. You have to switch on mentally, so that running becomes something you really want to do. If you adopt that attitude you will be changed and out in no time.

When you are feeling under pressure or anxious, promise yourself that at one o'clock, or whenever it is, you will be out in the park, feeling the breeze on your face, without having to worry about anything except yourself. It might even help to have a few mutters to put you into the right frame of mind, such as, 'Five o'clock is running time'; 'Running makes the heart grow stronger'; 'Running is fun, running is life'.

Think of the joys of being physically fit, in command, running easily between the trees. Even if you can't do it yet, you will soon if you try. As they say in the USA 'Tomorrow is the first day of the rest of your life', so now is the time to start. All you have to do is get out of the door. It doesn't matter if you have to turn back early, the thing is to get started then you'll be ahead of all those who are just thinking about it.

Having definite targets

Now you are out of the door, on your feet, and starting to jog. How far are you going to go? How fast are you going to run? When should you stop? Are you being over-cautious or over-ambitious? These questions are very difficult for the beginner to answer. It is for this reason that I have set out schedules in the succeeding chapters. You should always have some sort of target. When you get more experienced you can just say to yourself '20 minutes easy will be enough for today,' but the beginner must have a path of progression.

Start with the time spent on your feet. Even if you can't measure the distance, you can easily time the duration of your jog with a wristwatch – stopwatches are only for track specialists. Your targets should be to cover a minimum distance, or to go out for a minimum time, and it is usually a good thing to have a maximum too, otherwise your week may become unbalanced. If you have a target, and you keep to it, you have achieved something. You can record it, and then have something to build on. If you have no target, and don't know how much you have done, then your training will soon fade into a blur in your memory, and you won't know where to go next.

Measuring distances

The precise distance you run is really not all that important. Provided that you test yourself over the same courses you can check your improvement. However, if you want to compare your progress with absolute standards you should estimate the distances as closely as possible. The quickest way is to use the milometer on a car or cycle – one that measures in tenths of a mile. If you go round your course two or three times you will increase the accuracy of the measurement. If that is not possible, you could make your own measuring wheel, using an old cycle wheel, and count the number of revolutions as you push it round the course.

The next best way, and one that is quite accurate, is to use a pedometer. This will count the number of paces you take, but you have to know what your stride length is. To do this, walk around a running track (normally 400 meters or 436 yards) and count your strides, or walk along a beach, and then use a tape measure to measure, say, ten strides. If none of these things is possible, go to your nearest playing fields and ask the groundsman how long the football pitch is, then see how many strides you take for the length of the pitch. Once you know how many strides you take to a hundred yards you can pace out a course fairly accurately even without a pedometer.

The laziest way is to measure the courses on a map. You can buy the 2½ inch (1:25000) OS maps of your area, or you can go and look at the six-inch maps at the council surveyor's offices. These are accurate if used properly, but tend to give a slightly shorter distance than the ground you actually cover – at least that's what I like to think!

How to jog

You should not really need this section at all. Running is a perfectly natural action. If you watch children running you will see that their style is easy and relaxed. However, some adults have got so far away from the time when they used to run about that their ideals are confused by seeing track runners on television. The jogger's stride should be short, not lifting the knee very much, not coming down heavily, not landing with the feet flat.

In a natural jogging action the heel strikes the ground first and the weight is transferred along the outside of the foot, with the thrust coming from all the toes.

When you start, you will probably find it easiest to run 'on your heels' – that is, with your foot landing heel first. As your body comes forwards, putting the weight on to the front foot, the weight is transferred from the heel to the toe. Think of the outline of a bare foot in the sand. That is the way the weight is shifted, along the outside of the foot, then across to the ball of the foot, with the final push off the ground coming from all the toes together.

The rest of the body should be able to look after itself. You will soon find the running position which comes most naturally to you. Keep your back straight – this will allow your breathing muscles to work freely. If you lean forwards slightly this will keep your centre of gravity over your feet and prevent you from landing on your heels too heavily.

When you start to run a bit faster, you will find that your stride gets longer, your knees come up more, and you point

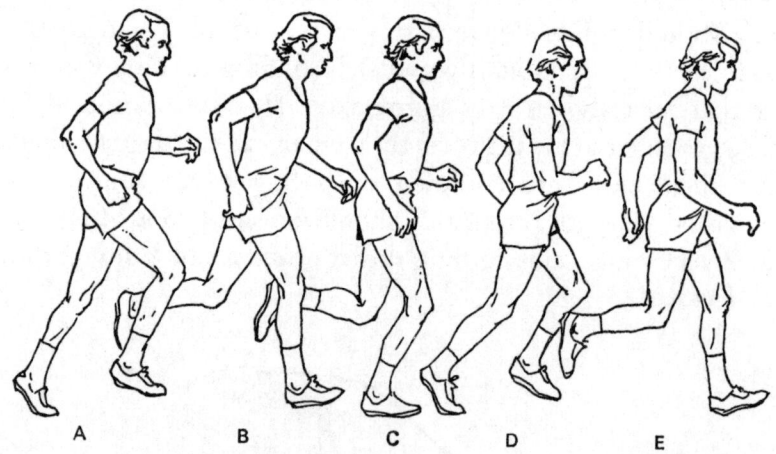

A   B   C   D   E

Good jogging action: (A) Upright body carriage, with head slightly in front of the point of balance and not too much knee lift. (B) Note the arms swinging loosely, with the hands at about waist level. The heel of the foot strikes the ground first. (C) The weight of the body is transferred in a rolling action along the foot. The knee bends to absorb the shock of landing. (D) The jogging stride is quite short: the left foot is on its way down as the toes on the right foot are pushing off. (E) The head and shoulders remain relaxed throughout. The heel does not come up very far behind. Run evenly, with the same amount of thrust from each foot – favouring one leg can lead to muscle problems.

your toe slightly as your foot comes down to the ground. This means that the ball of your foot will strike the ground first, and then you will go on to your heel, and rock forwards again. So the running action is ball-heel-ball-toes. Only when you are running really fast will you be running on your toes. This is the sprinter's action, and does not concern the jogger at all. Trying to run on your toes will only result in strained arches and stiff calf muscles.

How fast is jogging ?

The only difference between jogging and running is one of speed. A fast walk is about 4 miles an hour, after that you break into a slow jog, which is 5 or 6 miles an hour (or 10 to 12 minutes per mile). A normal jogging pace for most people is around 6 or 7 miles an hour and when you reach 8 miles an hour you can call it running. Most trained runners do their steady runs at 8 to 10 miles an hour (6 to 7½ minutes per mile), but their fast runs may be done at around 12 miles an hour (5 minutes per mile) or even faster. Although a 5 minute mile may seem impossible to the casual jogger, top class marathon runners can run 26 miles at this speed.

Warming up

If you have watched athletics on television you will have seen the athletes jogging round the track, warming-up for their event. Is this necessary for joggers? No, it isn't most of the time. Jogging is done at a slower speed than running, and it is non-competitive. You should start off at a nice comfortable pace, not sprint off, in fact you may even prefer to walk the first 50 yards.

You will find that the exercise becomes easier after the first five minutes, because it takes that time for your system to get adjusted to the extra demands being made upon it. If you have been sitting in a car, driving home, or sitting in your chair waiting for the chance to get out, it will take longer to adapt to the running movement, and you should start off even more slowly. After driving, in particular, your calf muscles may be rather tight, and you should give them time to ease out. Warming up becomes important only in the later stages of the schedules, when you are doing time trials and running at quite a fast speed, probably on a road or a track. If you try to run fast, from a sitting start, so to speak, you will not be as fast as you would if you preceeded the trial with five minutes of gentle jogging and some stretching and loosening exercise such as those described in Chapter 8.

Being warm is important. Cold muscles do not work as efficiently as warm muscles, so going out in just shorts and a T-shirt on a cold day is not really wise. It is better to put on too much clothing, some of which can be taken off later, than to put on too little and be cold and miserable throughout the run. You will get stiff much more quickly if you let yourself get cold.

The après-jog

You have done it. You have completed your mile, or your 20 minutes. You come in feeling warm, a little tired, and glowing with satisfaction. What next? Don't just collapse in a heap on to the sofa and call for a beer. If you do this you will cool down a lot as the sweat evaporates, and this may cause you to stiffen up. If possible the sequence of events should be: jog – shower – change – drink.

A warm shower is quicker and more refreshing than a bath. It is also cheaper and washes you more effectively. I don't see any virtue whatsoever in following up a run with a cold bath, unless you've been running in tropical conditions and really need to lower your body temperature. In normal circumstances a cold shower is likely to do more harm than good.

If you can't get a bath or shower after your run, then just walk around slowly, putting your track suit on again if you feel at all cold. The walking will produce a bit of heat, so that you don't cool too suddenly.

You will certainly lose some sweat while you are running

– when I was running across the Arizona desert I was losing at least a pint every two miles, For this reason it is a good thing to have a drink not long after you have finished. What you drink really doesn't matter very much, except that sweet drinks will tend to put back the calories you were hoping to lose. Being an Englishman, I think there is nothing to beat a nice cup of tea on most days, but I do like a beer in hot weather. It is not a good idea to have an ice-cold drink the moment you finish as this may upset your temperature-control system. The proprietary after-game drinks are expensive, and unnecessary for the casual jogger.

Try not to rush things after you have jogged. Make sure that you have somewhere to change and shower, and that you can do it calmly in ten minutes. If you try to pack too much into the time, and have to rush around faster than ever after you jog, you will lose the benefits. This is why I want you to integrate your running with your daily life, not just tack it on. By the time you have changed you will feel relaxed, pleasantly tired, at peace with yourself and ready to handle the next part of the day.

If you are going on to eat afterwards, don't gorge yourself, and don't eat junk food; eat something you like. When you go on to the rest of the day, make sure that you have the right clothing, so that you keep your equilibrium.

Keeping tabs

To get the best out of your jogging you have to be able to see the patterns. This means keeping a check, of the time you spend jogging, and the approximate distance covered. It is enough to make a single entry in a pocket diary, say: '21 minutes, 2 miles approx', At the end of each week tot up either the total time of the total distance covered.

Two other things you should keep a record of – your body weight and your resting pulse. Weigh yourself once a week, on the same scales, at the same time of day, and make a note of your weight. Check your pulse on waking up in the morning, about once a week, and make a note of that too. There are several other ways of assessing your physical condition but the jogger's motto should be 'Keep it simple.'

Starting a jogging group

Most things are more fun done with somebody else, and this goes for jogging too. If you can form a group you are more likely to keep up your intentions. The ways to get a group going are:

1 Talk to your friends and find the days and times which suit you all best.
2 Put up a card on your town/school/office/church notice board.
3 Ring up your local newspaper, or write to them. They will be happy to give you a paragraph or two.
4 Write to your regional sports council office. They should know of jogging groups in the area.
5 Write to your local health authority. They should have an interest in promoting jogging and will be able to advise anyone worried about their state of health.
6 Try the people who run keep-fit groups in the winter – they may be interested in jogging in the summer.

When you have got some other people interested, get going as soon as possible. You will find that there are many other people who are interested but haven't quite got the confidence to start on their own.

When you start to jog, fix a circular course and let everyone go round at their own pace. Be prepared to give advice when it is asked for, but don't force people into doing things against their will. Let things go along of their own accord. If there is sufficient support and enthusiasm after the first few weeks, you can think of taking part in fun-runs in the locality, or even of organizing your own.

4 The beginner's schedule

Who this is for

Anyone over 40 who has not jogged before.

Anyone over 30 who is neither doing an active sport once a week nor walking a mile a day regularly.

Anyone who is more than 14lb overweight, but not more than 40lb overweight. (Anyone more than 40lb overweight should see a doctor before starting an exercise programme.)

Anyone who has had a serious illness in the last six months and has since been pronounced healthy.

I should like to stress that once you are on to the right point on the schedules, age and sex don't come into it at all. A man of 35 who is overweight might find himself at the same point as a woman of 45 and a man of 55. What matters is your personal progression.

Long term goals

The object of the beginner's schedule is to build up all the aspects of your fitness, so that, whatever your initial level, you can reach the start of the regular jogging schedule. In terms of speed, the goals are: 1 mile in under 12 minutes; 2 miles in under 28 minutes; 4 miles in an hour. These targets are to be accomplished, not without effort, but without severe strain, before you can go on to the next schedule.

The beginner's time schedule at a glance

Miles	Weeks/stages					
	1	2	3	4	5	6
1	20	18	16	14	13	12
1½		30	27	24		21
2			36	32	30	28
3				48	44	40
4					65	60

The figures in the steps are the target times in minutes for each stage of fitness. You won't be going for target times or distances every day, but they are a guide as to what you should be able to achieve at each stage. The stages will only correspond with weeks if you manage to go through all six weeks without any troubles or interruptions.

The beginner's schedule: week 1

Objectives: To get out 4 times during the week.

To cover 1 mile in 20 minutes.

Day 1: Stroll gently for 10 minutes, then turn round and walk home briskly. No jogging today.

Day 2: Rest.

Day 3: Walk briskly along the route you covered on day 1. See how much further you get in 10 minutes. When you turn round, walk slowly to gather yourself together, then try a gentle trot for about 50 yards. Walk until you feel recovered, then try another gentle trot, for, say, 60 yards. If you feel alright, you can try this twice more, then walk the last ¼ mile home briskly.

Day 4: Rest.

Day 5: Find another place, preferably one which offers a circuit of 1 mile. Walk over the course without pushing yourself, striding out briskly in places and then just strolling along.

Day 6: Try to go the whole mile non-stop at a good walking pace, without breaking into a trot. If it is a measured mile, time yourself. If you can't measure the mile, see how far you can go on a 10 minutes out, 10 minutes back basis, and make a mental note of the distance you cover.

Day 7: Rest.

Comments on the first week

This is not meant to be a strenuous programme. It is designed to make sure that you can cover the distance before you start to speed up. There is not much 'heart training' involved here – that will come later. You must walk before you can run and the main thing is that you have made a start.

Progression

Week achieved without strain – proceed to week 2.

Week not completed for any reason – restart week 1.

Stiffness or aches in the legs on day 7 – repeat week 1.

Acute breathlessness during the brief periods of jogging – see a doctor.

The beginner's schedule: week 2

Objectives: To get out 4 times during the week.
To cover 1 mile in 18 minutes.

Day 1:   Go out to one of your 1-mile circuits, walking briskly
           most of the way, with short patches of gentle jogging.
           After 80–100 yards of jogging, walk slowly until your
           breathing is back to normal. The patterns therefore will
           be: 300 yards brisk walk, 100 yards jog, 50 yards slow
           walk, repeated 3 times.

Day 2:   Rest.

Day 3:   We are increasing the distance to 1½ miles, or about 30
           minutes if you are going on time rather than distance.
           Follow the same pattern as on day 1 but, if anything, do
           more walking and less jogging. Remember – train, don't
           strain.

Day 4:   Rest.

Day 5:   A 2-mile walk. This is going to take you about 40
           minutes, so give yourself plenty of time. It is too long to
           fit into the lunch hour. I suggest you find a different
           place from your 1-mile circuits. Time doesn't matter,
           just cover the distance with as little stopping as possible.

Day 6:   Rest.

Day 7:   A 1-mile brisk walk round the same circuit as in week 1.
           You should be able to do it in 18 minutes by steady
           walking, without needing either to stop or to jog.

Comments on the second week

So far the level of work has not been very intensive, and you
probably won't have worked hard enough to sweat. You can
wear ordinary clothing for these two weeks, but the third
week will introduce more jogging, so you should make sure
you have the right gear.

Progression

Week achieved without strain – proceed to week 3.
Week interrupted – repeat week 2.
Stiffness, with leg or foot trouble resulting – check that you
have the right kind of footwear, then restart week 1. It is vital

that your feet, legs and general system can take 2 miles of walking before we start on regular jogging.

Week achieved but day 7 was very hard work – repeat week 2.

The beginner's schedule : week 3

Objectives: To cover 6 miles during the week.

To cover 1 mile in 16 minutes.

Day 1: 1½ miles as last week, but try to fit in 6 periods of jogging, each one of 100 yards or more. If you are jogging really slowly, as you should at this stage, this means about 40 seconds of continuous jogging at a stretch.

Day 2: Rest.

Day 3: 2 miles today, but if you managed well last week you can afford to stride out more confidently. If you feel good, you can jog some short stretches in the middle, but walk the last ½ mile.

Day 4: Rest.

Day 5: 1½ miles again, but with a little more jogging. The pattern should now be: 200 yards brisk walking, 110 yards jogging, 50 yards slow walking, (or until your breathing is back to normal) repeated 6 times.

Day 6: Rest.

Day 7: 1 mile again. The target is now 16 minutes, which is either a fast walk all the way, or a steady walk with brief periods of jogging.

Comments on the third week

For the first time I have introduced heart training. The periods of jogging should make you warm and a bit breathless, and your pulse rate will go up. This is deliberate: you won't improve unless you put yourself under a little stress. However, it is essential to check your pulse, to make sure you aren't over-straining yourself. The figure for the maximum safe rate can be estimated by subtracting your age from 220, so if you are 40 you should not go over 180. If it is below 120 you will not get much benefit. When you are jogging, your pulse rate should be somewhere between 120 and 170. Individuals do differ a lot though: if you are feeling tired and breathless, although your pulse is only 155, you should not push yourself any harder. The effect of training can be achieved by reaching a state of mild discomfort – you should not be punishing yourself.

Progression
Week achieved without strain – proceed to week 4.
Week achieved, but failed to reach target time – repeat week 3.
Week achieved with a great deal of effort – repeat week 3.
Gave up during the week – go back to week 2.
Foot or leg troubles during the week – see Chapter 9.
Chest pains or breathing difficulties while jogging – see a doctor.

The beginner's schedule: week 4

Objectives: To cover 6 miles or more in the week.
　　　　　　To cover 1 mile in 14 minutes.

Day 1:　　2 or 3 miles walking. Keep up a good speed and don't stop at all. You may jog for brief periods on the flat or downhill.

Day 2:　　Rest.

Day 3:　　1½ miles, as in the previous week, with about 250 yards of walking to 110 yards of jogging.

Day 4:　　Rest.

Day 5:　　As day 3. To avoid monotony, choose a different route, but keep to the same pattern.

Day 6:　　Rest, or 1 mile easy walk.

Day 7:　　The mile trial again. Aim at achieving it in under 14 minutes.

Comments on the fourth week
This is a crucial stage in the programme. The previous weeks may not have seemed very hard, except for the mental effort of getting out, which is not to be ignored. The pattern of this week is the same as that of week 3, so that you get used to a regular dose of jogging. After two weeks of this you should be getting the benefits, and your general system should have toughened up considerably. Most adults under the age of 60 can do 1 mile in 16 minutes, with varying degrees of discomfort, but to do it in a faster time is more demanding, and really unfit

people just can't manage it. If you have followed the programme properly, however, you will be able to run 1 mile in under 14 minutes without any trouble.

Progression
Week achieved without strain – proceed to week 5.
Week achieved ,with a lot of effort – repeat week 4.
Gave up during the week – go back to week 3.
Week achieved, but failed to reach target – repeat week 4.
Foot or leg troubles during the week – see Chapter 9.

The beginner's schedule: week 5

Objectives: To cover 8 miles during the week.
          To cover 2 miles in under 30 minutes.

Day 1:   Walk 3 miles briskly. This should not take much more than 45 minutes now that you have four weeks of training behind you.

Day 2:   Rest.

Day 3:   1 to 2 miles of walking and jogging. The distance jogged should now be almost as great as the distance walked, so that the pattern will now be: 150 yards brisk walk, 150 yards jogging, 50 yards slow walk (or until your breathing is back to normal), repeated 4 times over 1 mile. Remember to use the pulse rate as a guide to how fast you go. You can start again when your pulse is below 120 and your breathing is normal.

Day 4:   Rest.

Day 5:   As day 3, but the two days need total only 3 miles.

Day 6:   Rest.

Day 7:   A trial over 2 miles. Use your 1-mile circuit and go round it twice. This will enable you to judge whether you are going at the right speed. This should be no problem to you now, but it will give you the confidence to go faster next week.

Comments on the fifth week
The training is a little harder this week. The total distance is a little greater due to that 3-mile walk, but more important, there is a higher proportion of jogging to walking in the two

middle days. The 2-mile trial may seem rather too easy – but look back to week 1. Could you have done it then? I have not made it faster because one must not increase the total week's training too sharply.

Progression
Week achieved without strain – proceed to week 6.
Gave up during week for physical reasons – go back to week 4.
Week interrupted, for other reasons – repeat week 5.
Week achieved, with a lot of effort – repeat week 5.

The beginner's schedule: week 6

Objectives: 1 mile in 12 minutes.
4 miles in an hour.

Day 1: Go out and walk 4 miles briskly. You are now quite fit enough to do this in an hour. Try to find somewhere pleasant to do it, so that you don't get bored .

Day 2: Rest.

Day 3: 1 to 2 miles walking and jogging. Follow the same pattern as last week, but increase the length of the jogging sections and the walking sections, so that the pattern is: walk 200 yards, jog 200 yards, walk 50 yards slowly, walk 150 yards briskly, jog 200 yards, and so on. In this way, you will do 4 200-yard jogs per mile, giving you a useful heart-training effect, and taking you a little further than week 5.

Day 4: Rest.

Day 5: As day 3, except that the two days together need not total more than 3 miles.

Day 6: Rest.

Day 7: Test your speed per 1 mile. The target is 12 minutes. Aim to walk briskly and jog short stretches, then drop back to a brisk walk.

Comments on the sixth week

If you are in the category that really needed to start with this schedule, you will find it quite hard to make the target time in the sixth week. You will almost certainly need to repeat the week's training at least once, before you can make it. Remember, the target time should not be achieved by a superhuman effort – this would give a false idea of your fitness. As your heart strengthens you will find it easier to keep up a steady jog, and what was previously impossible will become quite easy. That is what is so satisfying about this kind of training – you can really feel yourself improve.

Progression

This depends on how far you want to go. If you can maintain the level of fitness you have now reached you will at least have halted the degeneration process. If you carry on walking and jogging on the lines of week 5 and 6 you will gradually get a little bit fitter, but if you want to make any real progress you should go on to the basic jogging schedule in the next chapter.

5 The basic jogging schedule

Who this is for

Anyone under 30 who is not more than 14lb overweight.
Anyone over 30 who is already either doing an active sport once a week or walking a mile a day regularly.

Who this is not for

Anyone who is more than 14lb overweight. Anyone who has had a serious illness in the last six months.

I must repeat that once you have the right place for yourself in these programmes, age and sex do not come into it. There are plenty of men and women in their 50s, for whom the week 10 schedule in this chapter would be very easy. The only thing that should matter to you is steady personal improvement.

Long term goals

The object of this schedule is to develop your physical fitness to a point where you can cope easily with the stresses and strains of life. By becoming a successful jogger you will make yourself physiologically younger. The targets are: a mile in $7\frac{1}{2}$ minutes; 2 miles in 17 minutes; 5 miles in under an hour.

The steps to fitness

Increasing speed and heart fitness: as your heart gets stronger, you will be able to run at faster speeds with the same effort, and you will take less time to cover a mile.

```
12* _____5 mph
   11*
      10*_____6 mph
            9*
               8½*_____7 mph
                     8*
                              7½* 8 mph
```

*Minutes per mile

Increasing stamina: as your strength and endurance develop, you will be able to run longer distances without strain.

Week/Stage	Longest distance jogged continuously	Week/Stage	Longest distance jogged continuously
1	400 yd	6	2 miles
2	1 mile	7	3 miles
3	1½ miles	8	3 miles
4	2 miles	9	4 miles
5	2 miles	10	4 miles

The basic jogging schedule at a glance in minutes

Weeks/stages	1	2	3	4	5	6	7	8	9	10
1 mile	12	11	10		9	8½		8		7½
1½ miles			16	15		14	13		12	
2 miles				21	20	19		18		17
3 miles					34	32	31	30	29	28
4 miles								44	42	40
5 miles									57	54

Heart fitness, strength and stamina go side by side. Don't push one aspect and neglect the other. It will not be possible to do trials at all these distances each week, but they are a guide to what you ought to be able to achieve, without undue strain, at each stage of your progress.

Weeks will only correspond to stages if you are able to go right through the schedule without having to repeat a week. Many will find that a week has to be repeated once or twice, before the target time can be achieved.

A word to the younger and more active

The first weeks of this schedule may seem too easy if you can jog 1 mile in under 10 minutes with no trouble. I still recommend you to work through all the weeks, but you can make short cuts by skipping the rest days if you want to.

A word to the older and less active

The key to success is to progress steadily at the pace which suits you. Sometimes you will find that there is a long jog on day 1 of one week, directly after a time trial on day 7 of the week before. If you don't feel ready for it, just delay the start of the next week for a day.

Basic jogging schedule: week 1

Objectives: To cover at least 6 miles during the week.
To walk for an hour continuously.

Day 1: Go out on a circuit of 1 mile, or else go out for 6 minutes before turning round and coming home. Alternate walking 100 yards briskly with jogging gently for 100 yards. Repeat 7 times.

Day 2: Rest.

Day 3: Another mile, but this time increase the distance jogged to about 200 yards. Walk until your breathing is quite back to normal, then repeat. Aim to do 4 200-yard stretches of jogging.

Day 4: Rest.

Day 5: Walk 3 miles briskly, or for an hour if you go on time rather than distance.

Day 6:   1 to 1½ miles of jogging and walking. Keep the jog slow,
           but try to jog continuously for over 2 minutes each
           time (about 300–400 yards), then walk until recovered.
Day 7:   Rest.

Comments on the first week
Congratulations on getting started. It doesn't matter how fast
or how slow you jog at first, as long as you get yourself moving.
The speed will come later. Make sure that your jogging action
is as relaxed and natural as possible.

Progression
Week achieved without strain – proceed to week 2.
Week not achieved, or only with effort – go to beginner's
schedule, Chapter 4.
Feet or legs ache – check your footwear.

The basic jogging schedule: week 2
Objectives: To go out 4 times during the week.
           To cover 1 mile in 11 minutes.
Day 1:   1 or 2 miles of jogging and walking, as in day 6 of last
           week. You should be able to jog slowly for 400 yards, or
           2 minutes, without stopping. Repeat 4 or 5 times.
Day 2:   Rest.
Day 3:   As day 1, but try a different route. You can tell whether
           you are judging your speeds right by checking your pulse
           rate at the end of each jog. It should not be above 27
           beats in 10 seconds (162 a minute) when you stop, and
           you should not start again until it is below 20 beats per
           10 seconds.
Day 4:   Rest.
Day 5:   A stamina session: 3 miles or an hour of steady walking,
           with brief jogs on the downhill stretches if you feel like
           it.
Day 6:   Rest.
Day 7:   Your first trial, but it shouldn't be too hard. Find a
           1-mile course (4 laps of a track). Jog slowly and
           continuously, but allow yourself to walk if you get very
           breathless. Aim at 11 minutes or less.

Comments on the second week
If you have measured your mile accurately this trial will tell
you where you stand with regard to heart fitness. If you
managed, say, 8 minutes 50 seconds, without strain, you are
obviously quite fit and can move on to week 6 straight away.
It is better, however, to err on the side of caution. You may,
for example, be quite strong in the legs and able to cope with
the walking sections easily, but lacking in heart fitness, or vice
versa. Therefore, don't start a new week or stage unless you can
cope with all the days without strain.

Progression
Week achieved without strain:
1 mile in over 10 minutes 15 seconds – proceed to week 3.
1 mile in under 10 minutes 15 seconds but over 9 minutes
30 seconds – proceed to week 4.
1 mile in under 9 minutes 30 seconds but over 9 minutes –
proceed to week 5.
1 mile in under 9 minutes – proceed to week 6.
Week achieved but only with great effort – repeat week 2.
Gave up during the week – go back to week 1.
Foot or leg trouble during week – see Chapter 9.

Basic jogging schedule : week 3

Objectives: To go out 4 times during the week.
　　　　　　To cover 1 mile in under 10 minutes.

Day 1:　　Go round your 1½-mile course, jogging for four
　　　　　　2-minute periods interrupted by walking periods of
　　　　　　one minute, 45 seconds and 30 seconds. Walk or jog the
　　　　　　last few yards home.

Day 2:　　Rest.

Day 3:　　A 2-mile session. Try jogging continuously on the
　　　　　　outward mile, turn for home, walk a little, then come
　　　　　　back jogging most of the way, with short, walking
　　　　　　stretches only when you are getting breathless or you
　　　　　　think your pulse rate is getting too high.

Day 4:　　Rest.

Day 5:　　Another step forward: try to jog the whole 1½-mile
　　　　　　circuit continuously. Don't be proud about it, however,
　　　　　　if you are getting really tired or breathless, slow down
　　　　　　and walk for a few yards. It is gradual and continuous
　　　　　　improvement that we are after, not records.

Day 6:　　Rest.

Day 7:　　Aim to cover 1 mile in 10 minutes. Try to keep to as
　　　　　　steady a pace as possible.

Comments on the third week

There is a considerable stepping-up this week in terms of speed.
This will be taken very easily by some, but not by others
because the basic schedule covers a wide age and ability range.
If, for example, you can't jog for 1 mile non-stop, you will
have to stay on this week, or even go back to week 2, until your
system adjusts itself. Remember the jogger's motto is 'Train,
don't strain.'

Progression

Week achieved without strain – proceed to week 4.
Week achieved, but target not achieved – repeat week 3.
Week achieved only with much effort – repeat week 3.
Gave up during the week – go back to week 2.

Basic jogging schedule : week 4

Objectives: To cover 1½ miles in 15 minutes.

To cover 7 miles during the week.

Day 1: A 2-mile session, similar to last week's keeping within your abilities, jogging most of the time, but allowing yourself to ease up when necessary.

Day 2: Rest.

Day 3: A 15-minute or 1½-mile lap, done on a fast-and-slow basis. Jog briskly for 2 minutes, then walk for 50 yards or so until your breathing is back to normal. Repeat this 4 or 5 times. If it gets too tiring, cut down the brisk jogging periods to 1 minute each.

Day 4. Rest.

Day 5: Do 20 minutes or 2 miles of really slow jogging: try not to stop at all.

Day 6: A trial over 1½ miles. Aim at 15 minutes. The speed is no faster than you ran last week, and with the extra training you have been doing the extra ½ mile should be within your powers.

Day 7: Rest.

Comments on the fourth week

Here we are consolidating the previous week, without increasing the speed, but increasing the distance of continuous jogging. The fourth week may be the one in which you really start to feel good, or it may be the one in which aches and pains give problems if there is something wrong with either your footwear or your jogging action.

Progression

Week achieved without strain – proceed to week 5.

Week achieved only with much effort – repeat week 4.

Gave up for physical reasons – go back to week 3.

Gave up for other reasons – repeat week 4.

Foot or leg troubles – see Chapter 9.

Basic jogging schedule: week 5

Objectives: To cover 1 mile in 9 minutes.

To cover 8 miles during the week.

Day 1: A stamina session, which will take you about 35 minutes. You are going to cover 3 miles, jogging most of the way, but stopping to walk when you feel you need to. This may feel hard at first, but it is a necessary platform for the training ahead.

Day 2: Rest.

Day 3: A 1-mile or 2-mile session, based on the fast-and-slow principle, as explained last week. Use your pulse rate as a guide to the speed you should go during the fast sections.

Day 4: Rest.

Day 5: A 2-mile session of jogging: don't stop – if you need to, slow down.

Day 6: Rest.

Day 7: Another trial over 1 mile. This time the target is 9 minutes. You may like to do a little bit of jogging to warm up first, and some walking afterwards is advisable.

Comments on the fifth week

Three weeks ago you could not get near 10 minutes, and now I am asking you to go under 9 minutes. By this time, I would expect that the training you have been doing is having a positive effect, and you should see a considerable inprovement on the time of two weeks ago. However, it may take longer than this to improve by as much as a minute a mile, which is a big step.

Progression

Week achieved without strain – proceed to week 6.

Week achieved, but target time not reached – repeat week 5.

Gave up during week – go back to week 4.

Basic jogging schedule : week 6

Objective: To cover 2 miles in 19 minutes.

Day 1:   A repeat of last week. Go out over the same 3-mile course. You should have more confidence than last week that you can get round, so you can afford to rest a little less and move a little faster.

Day 2:   Rest.

Day 3:   A fast-and-slow session over 1½ miles. During the faster periods of jogging you should be covering 300 or 400 yards, then slowing down to a walk or a very slow jog, until your breathing is normal and your pulse rate is below 120 a minute.

Day 4:   Rest.

Day 5:   A continuous but slow jog over 2 miles, or a little more, taking over 20 minutes.

Day 6:   Rest.

Day 7:   A 2-mile trial. Go round your circuit of 1 mile twice, or use the course you have been using for 2-mile jogs. Aim for 19 minutes. If you achieved under 9 minutes for a mile last week you will be surprised how easy a 9½-minute mile feels.

Comments on sixth week

The pattern of the weeks is now settling down, with a stamina session, a fast-and-slow session, and a continuous jog. Each of these things helps you in a different way. Accurate measurement of time and distance is necessary only for the weekly trial.

Progression

Week achieved without strain – proceed to week 7.
Week achieved only with great effort – repeat week 6.
Week achieved, but not target time – repeat week 6.
Foot or leg trouble during the week – see Chapter 9.

Basic jogging schedule: week 7

Objective: To cover 1½ miles in 13 minutes.

Day 1: 3 miles. Speed does not really matter for this session which should test your stamina. If you feel good, do more at the same speed. If you feel bad, just get round the course slowly.

Day 2: Rest.

Day 3: A 2-mile fast-and-slow run. If you use the same route every week, you will find it mentally easier to have certain fixed points between which you jog fast, and then go as slowly as you like until you are recovered and ready for the next burst.

Day 4: Rest.

Day 5: A 2-mile steady pace jog, preferably over a different route from day 3. Alternatively you can just do 10 minutes jogging in any direction, turn round and come back.

Day 6: Rest.

Day 7: A trial over 1½ miles. Aim at 13 minutes. This means a pace slightly faster than 9 minutes per mile. Remember, keeping to a steady pace throughout is the most efficient way of achieving target time.

Comments on the seventh week

You may wonder why I recommend fast-and-slow runs in training, when a steady pace is more efficient. This is because it is only by the fast-and-slow method that you can get used to a quicker tempo, which will play a valuable part in the heart training. It is the same as interval training, which is used by all international athletes, and their bodies work on just the same principles as yours.

Progression

Week achieved without strain – proceed to week 8.
Week achieved only with great effort – repeat week 7.
Training done, but failed target time – repeat week 7.
Gave up, for physical reasons – go back to week 6.
Gave up for other reasons – repeat week 7.

Basic jogging schedule: week 8

Objective: To cover 1 mile in 8 minutes.

Day 1: Another step up in distance. I want you to do 4 miles, jogging and walking. Make sure you have the right protective footwear, especially if you are running on roads.

Day 2: Rest.

Day 3: 3 miles at a steady pace. If this is accurately measured and timed, you should be covering it in around 30 minutes.

Day 4: Rest.

Day 5: A 2-mile run, as last week.

Day 6: Rest.

Day 7: A trial over 1 mile. You have not done this for 3 weeks, so you should be a lot fitter and stronger than when you last attempted it. Aim at 8 minutes – this is 2 minutes per $\frac{1}{4}$-mile lap, if you are running on a standard track.

Comments on the eighth week

Another significant step forward here, in terms of quality. A mile in 8 minutes is definitely running rather than jogging, and if you reach this standard you can afford to congratulate yourself. Part of your improvement will come from finding out that you can stand a bit more discomfort than you thought you could. If you measure your pulse rate just after finishing your trial, it will give you an idea of how hard you are pushing yourself. The maximum safe level is a rate per minute of 220 minus your age.

Progression

Week achieved without strain – proceed to week 9.

Week achieved only with an effort – repeat week 8.

Training done, but failed target time – repeat week 8.

Gave up during the week – go back to week 7.

Basic jogging schedule: week 9

Objectives: To cover 5 miles in under an hour.

To cover $7\frac{1}{2}$ miles in 12 minutes.

Day 1: 5 miles of jogging and walking. If you jog most of the way and only walk the uphill stretches, you will be well under the hour. Try to find a pleasant area, park or woodland.

Day 2: Rest.

Day 3: 2 miles jogging and walking briskly. This should seem nothing after your five-mile effort.

Day 4: Rest.

Day 5: 2 or 3 miles of fast and slow training. Try to do $\frac{1}{2}$-mile at a good speed, then cut down to doing bursts of 300 to 400 yards.

Day 6: Rest.

Day 7: A trial over $1\frac{1}{2}$ miles. You are going at the same speed as last week, but for 12 minutes instead of 8 minutes. Whether you can manage it depends on how quickly you are responding to the training. You can expect it to take longer if you are over 40.

Comments on the ninth week

You have now reached the maximum distance you are expected to run in these schedules, 10 to 12 miles a week. The 5-mile session will take up more time than the average jog, and can probably be done best at weekends. A good way of making sure you do it is to be dropped 5 miles from home!

Progression

Week achieved without strain – proceed to week 10.

Week achieved only with great effort – repeat week 9.

Target time not achieved – repeat week 9.

Gave up during the week – go back to week 8.

Basic jogging schedule : week 10

Objective: To jog 4 miles in 40 minutes.

To jog 2 miles in 17 minutes.

Day 1: 4 miles of steady jogging. The pace needed is only 10 minutes a mile, so it should come more easily than the 8-minute mile you have just been doing.

Day 2: Rest.

Day 3: 2 miles varying the pace. Start easily, then do bursts of 200–300 yards, with about 100 yards of very slow jogging between each.

Day 4: Rest.

Day 5: 2 or 3 miles, including two long stretches at a sustained pace, about 4 minutes each, then running steadily home.

Day 6: Rest.

Day 7: The last trial. Go over either your 2-mile or your 1-mile course. The target times are 17 minutes and $7\frac{1}{2}$ minutes respectively. Loosen up properly before you start, particularly for the mile, which is at a faster pace than anything you have done before.

Comments on the tenth week

The 4- and 5-mile sessions of the past three weeks will put more strain on your joints and supporting muscles, but these should have been built up sufficiently in the previous weeks to be able to take it. If you do feel strains in your ankles or knees after these long sessions, and they are not recovered 48 hours later, give yourself another day or two's rest before going on with the schedule. It is better to rest a day than to go on pushing yourself and lose two or three weeks due to an injury. It also does your image no good if you are limping about with a strained knee – you can expect no sympathy from your inactive friends.

You will have noticed that the last few weeks have become rather similar in what is recommended. This is because you are reaching a plateau of fitness, where further improvement is not called for. If you can manage one 4-mile run and three 2-mile runs during the week, you will maintain an excellent standard of fitness and your weight will gradually come down, provided you also pay attention to the diet chapter. If you do the long jog at the weekends, you need only take two or three 20-minutes jogs in your working week to stay in shape. You will naturally establish a regular routine, of the kind you have been doing in the last three weeks.

Where do you go from here?

When you have achieved all the targets in week 10, go on to the complete jogger's schedule, which will give you something to aim at all the year round, with slightly different patterns for different times of the year. If you are still more ambitious, you will find more advice at the end of that chapter. If you have come this far with me, congratulations! I hope that you are really enjoying it now. It should be a part of your life that you cannot do without.

6 The complete jogger's schedule

Introduction

I am assuming that you are now sold on the benefits of jogging and know how to go about it. You have worked your way through the basic schedule to a point where you are no longer improving in the time which you can afford. Where do you go from here? If you were really determined to get a lot better you could go on to a real runner's training programme, but that implies 5 hours or more a week, as against the $1\frac{1}{2}$ hours required by these schedules. You could just go on repeating the last two weeks, but that might become tedious. What I have devised is a set of maintenance schedules that will keep you in good shape throughout the year, but with slightly different stresses according to the seasons. The winter schedule could also be used in unfavourable conditions – for example, during the rainy season in a tropical country, or when you are under pressure at work and have time only for the absolute minimum. The spring and autumn schedules are the biggest ones, and could be used when you are really determined to get yourself into a high state of fitness, or happen to have the time to spare.

Because these schedules will be followed by people of different ability, it will not be possible to specify times, except for those who have gone through to week 10 of the basic schedule. For those worthy people, the targets are set out in the complete jogger's schedule.

The complete jogger's time schedule at a glance

	Basic schedule				Complete schedule			
Weeks/stages	7	8	9	10	+1	+2	+3	+4
1 mile		8		7½			7	6¾
1½ miles	13		12		11½		11	10½
2 miles		18		17		16		15
3 miles	31	30	29	28	27	26	25	24
4 miles		44	42	40	38	36	35	34
5 miles			57	54	52	50	48	46
6 miles						66	63	60

The winter schedule

When to use it:

When the weather is bad.

When you are really short of time.

When you have spent at least eight weeks on the basic schedule.

When you have got at least as far as the end of week 6.

The winter schedule: week 1

Objective: 60 minutes of jogging or equivalent brisk exercise per week.

Day 1: 2 miles or 20 minutes of slow, continuous jogging. You can do this anywhere – 10 minutes trotting slowly along a road, and 10 minutes back.

Day 2: Rest.

Day 3: 2 miles or 20 minutes of fast-and-slow jogging. Jog briskly for a minute or 200 yards, then slow down to a gentle trot for another 200 yards. Repeat 7 times.

Day 4: Rest.

Day 5: Twice round a 1-mile circuit. Jog easily the first time round; allow a minute or two to recover before going round again fast and timing yourself. This is the only rigorous bit of the schedule, and the only guide to your fitness, so do it properly.

Days 6 and 7: Rest (but see Chapter 7 on how to stay fit when you have no time at all for training).

The winter schedule: week 2

Objective: Four 15-minute sessions per week, indoors or outdoors.

Day 1: 1½ miles or 15 minutes of steady jogging.

Day 2: Rest.

Day 3: 15 minutes of indoor 'heart training' exercise using for example a skipping rope, a static bicycle or a rowing machine, or stepping on and off a bench. Use the 'fast-and-slow' principle – 2 minutes steady, 6 fast minutes, interspersed with 6 slow minutes, then 1 minute steady pace.

Day 4: Rest.

Day 5: Time trial over either the 1-mile or the 1½-mile course. Make sure that you are warm before starting.

Day 6: Rest.

Day 7: 15 to 20 minutes of gym work, preferably circuit training or light-weight training. Use as wide a range of exercises as possible and don't take on heavy weights or strenuous exercises if you are not used to them.

WINTER   SUMMER

The jogger for all seasons: in winter keeping yourself warm is what matters; in summer you should avoid overheating.

Comments on the winter schedule

You should have enough experience of my schedules by now to be able to adapt the material of these two weeks according to your circumstances. It is important to give yourself a trial at least every two weeks to reassure yourself about your state of fitness. This schedule, if maintained, will in fact keep you in reasonable condition indefinitely. You won't go back from where you were before, but you won't go forward either. Remember that if you are doing this schedule because of lack of time, you will already be under strain, and the jogging is meant to lessen the strain, not increase it. Make an effort to set aside the necessary time and then work through your schedule without rushing it. Be sure you have read the sections on warming up and cold weather precautions beforehand.

The spring schedule

When to use it:
When you are building up to a new peak of fitness.
When you are preparing for a challenge.
When you have been on the winter schedule and want to raise your level.

Long term goals:
To run 10 miles per week.
To improve your best run over 3 miles.

The spring schedule: weeks 1 to 4

This is a preparatory period. If you are going into this regime after the winter schedule, or a period of less activity, you will have to regain your previous level of fitness before starting anything more strenuous. How far you have to go depends on how far you have let yourself go.

If you have stuck to the winter schedule, I suggest that you repeat the last two weeks that you managed of the basic schedule.
If you had previously reached week 10, repeat weeks 9 and 10.
If you had previously reached week 7, repeat weeks 6 and 7.
If you are not sure of your physical state, go back to repeat the last four weeks of the basic schedule.
If you have not yet reached week 10 of the basic schedule, refer back to it and carry on. When you have done week 10 of the basic schedule you may start on week 5 of the complete jogger's spring schedule.

The spring schedule: week 5

Objectives: 10 miles in the week.

$1\frac{1}{2}$ miles in 11 minutes and 30 seconds.

Day 1: 3 miles at a steady pace, slowing down if necessary but without stopping.

Day 2: Rest.

Day 3: A brisk 2 miles. Start slowly, then keep up as fast a pace as is comfortable and jog the last few hundred yards slowly.

Day 4: Rest.

Day 5: A trial over 3 miles. Aim at 27 minutes. As this is only 9 minutes per mile, it should not be too difficult, but don't start too fast.

Day 6: Rest.

Day 7: 1 or $1\frac{1}{2}$ miles against the clock. We are now going at a running speed, rather than just jogging, so you will need at least $\frac{1}{2}$ mile to warm up, plus some stretching, before attempting the trial. Aim at 11 minutes 30 seconds for $1\frac{1}{2}$ miles, or else improve your previous best mile time.

The spring schedule: week 6

Objective: 2 miles in 10 minutes.

Day 1: 4 miles, taken slowly and easily. You can spend as long as you like over this – it is a stamina session – but you should be jogging rather than walking.

Day 2: Rest.

Day 3: 2 miles of fast-and-slow training. Make the fast periods 200–400 yards, and the slow periods 100–200 yards, or as long as it takes to get your breath back.

Day 4: Rest.

Day 5: A 2-mile session. Jog the first $\frac{1}{2}$ mile slowly, run the next mile briskly, then slow down for the last $\frac{1}{2}$ mile.

Day 6: Rest.

Day 7: A trial over 2 miles. Aim at 16 minutes. This means warming up beforehand, and going through the first mile feeling that you still have something in hand.

The spring schedule: week 7

Objective: 3 miles in 25 minutes.

Day 1:   3 miles slowly or 30 minutes. As you had a hard run yesterday, you can afford to take it gently. Don't worry about the time.

Day 2:   Rest.

Day 3:   2 miles at a good brisk pace. You are now quite fit enough to do 2 miles in well under 20 minutes without taking too much out of yourself.

Day 4:   Rest.

Day 5:   2 miles alternately fast and slow, as last week.

Day 6:   Rest.

Day 7:   A 3-mile trial. This is getting harder, deliberately so. You will not be running at a very fast pace – about $8\frac{1}{2}$ minutes per mile – but it will require mental effort to keep this pace going all the way. Still, it is worth the effort. You are making yourself a better runner every week.

The spring schedule: week 8

Objective: 2 miles in 15 minutes or 3 miles in 24 minutes.

Day 1:   A 3-mile, easy jog, as last week.

Day 2:   Rest.

Day 3:   3 miles of fast-and-slow training. As you get tired, cut down on the distances of the fast bursts, rather than lengthen the recovery period. If you are worried, check your pulse before starting the fast sections.

Day 4:   Rest.

Day 5:   A brisk 2 miles. If you are feeling the effects of the past few days of training, you may take it easy.

Day 6:   Rest.

Day 7:   Warm up over $\frac{1}{2}$ mile, then test your speed over 2 or 3 miles. Again we are trying for something you would have considered impossible a few weeks ago, but by your consistent training you have now made it possible. The speed is no faster than you have done before over shorter distances, and you should have gained the extra endurance over the last few weeks.

Comments on the spring schedule
This is the hardest training you will find in this book. Anything harder than this takes you out of the realms of the keep-fit jogger and into real running. In the last four weeks of training given above, the demands made increased quite sharply, and it will often take two or three weeks to achieve the target times given. If you have kept hard at it for eight weeks or so, and want something to take you further, go on to the end of this chapter.

The summer schedule

When to use it:
When the weather is warm.
When you have beaches or grass to run on.
When you are doing other sports.
When you want to step up the speed of your running.
After any of the spring, autumn or winter schedules.

Long term goals:
1 mile in under 7 minutes
1½ miles in 10 minutes 30 seconds.

Given that one of the objects of the whole business is enjoyment, this schedule should be more fun than any of the others. It is quite strenuous, but doesn't take long. The pleasure of striding along a firm beach in the sunshine, feeling your body moving smoothly, and knowing that you are in good shape, make it really worth doing.

Weeks 1 and 2 are preparatory weeks, intended for anyone who has come direct from the winter schedule, or is between weeks 6 and 10 of the basic schedule. If you have finished week 10 of the basic schedule, or have been doing the spring or autumn schedules, you should start on week 3.

The summer schedule: week 1

Objective: To get out four times during the week.

Day 1: 1 mile only, or 10 minutes. Find a nice place, such as a stretch of beach, a cricket field, a park, or the edge of a golf course. It need not be large, but large enough to give you at least $\frac{1}{4}$ mile of running. A beach 200 yards long or a field 100 yards square is big enough. If it is nice enough to be able to run on it in bare feet, so much the better as this will help considerably to firm up your muscles. Having found your patch, jog around it for 10 minutes, starting very slowly and increasing speed gradually.

Day 2: Jog 400 yards slowly, then speed up for 100 yards, then slow down until you get your breath back. Repeat this until you have done $\frac{1}{2}$ mile, then do 200 yards fast jog, 200 yards slow jog, 200 fast, 200 slow, and finish with the last $\frac{1}{4}$ mile at an easy pace. The total of $1\frac{1}{2}$ miles should take you less than 20 minutes.

Day 3: Rest.

Day 4: A 1-mile session. Start with 200 or 300 yards of easy jogging, until you feel loose, then alternate 100 yards of striding out with an equal distance of easy jogging, and repeat this six times. In two or three of the fast stretches, try picking your knees up a bit more and getting up on to your toes. You will have to use a more vigorous arm action.

Day 5: Rest.

Day 6: $1\frac{1}{2}$ miles of brisk jogging. Don't worry about the time, but it will be no more than 15 minutes.

Day 7: Rest.

The summer schedule: week 2

Day 1: 1 mile, or 10 minutes, as day 4 of last week. Once again try and get up on to your toes for a few strides, but if you are getting pain in your toes, or in the arch of your foot, go back to the usual action.

Day 2: Rest.

Day 3: 2 miles of fast-and-slow training. Make your fast

stretches about 200 yards. If you jog slowly afterwards, you should recover in a further 200 yards. Repeat four times, then cut down to 100 yards fast, 100 yards slow, until you have run 2 miles or 20 minutes.

Day 4:   Rest.
Day 5:   1 mile slow and easy, just fast enough to get warm. This will help to overcome the stiffness you may get from doing fast work.
Day 6:   Rest.
Day 7:   Jog for ¼ mile; move fast for ½ mile, then jog slowly another ¼ mile.

The summer schedule: weeks 3 and 4

Objectives: To get used to running faster.
           To improve your time over 1 mile.

The summer schedule: week 3

Day 1:   Find an area with a good running surface (see week 1). Do 15 minutes of easy jogging, interspersed with fast bursts of about 100 yards each. Get your arms working and get up on to your toes as you accelerate then slow down gradually.
Day 2:   Rest.
Day 3:   A 1-mile session. Jog the first 200 or 300 yards easily, then gradually increase your speed until you are working as fast as is comfortable. Keep this going for about ½ mile, then jog the last few hundred yards easily. Alternatively jog out from home easily for 5 minutes, then run fast all the way back.
Day 4:   Rest.
Day 5:   A 15-minute steady run, or some other mildly strenuous sport, such as a swim or a game of tennis.
Day 6:   Rest.
Day 7:   ½-mile easy jog, followed by a fast mile, against the clock if you have the opportunity. It should be as fast as your previous best, which is 7 minutes 30 seconds, or better, if you have gone past week 10.

The summer schedule: week 4

Day 1:   Rest.
Day 2:   2 miles of fast-and-slow training. After an easy jog, follow the same pattern as day 3 of week 2.
Day 3:   Rest.
Day 4:   1 mile of fast-and-slow training, with the fast bursts of no more than 100 yards. Try to accelerate smoothly, gradually getting further up on to your toes and increasing the length of your stride. Hold your maximum speed for about 30 yards, then slow down gradually, and jog slowly until ready for the next burst.
Day 5:   1 mile of easy jogging or some other sport.
Day 6:   Rest.
Day 7:   Warm up over $\frac{1}{2}$ mile. Do a time trial over 1 or $1\frac{1}{2}$ miles. Your target times are 7 minutes and 11 minutes respectively.

The summer schedule: weeks 5 and 6

Objectives: To be able to run fast and enjoy it.
To improve your time over 1 mile still further.

The summer schedule: week 5

Day 1:   1 mile of fast-and-slow, as day 4 of last week.
Day 2:   Rest.
Day 3:   2 miles of fast-and-slow, as previously described, but increasing the length of the fast bursts to 300 yards, or 1 minute.
Day 4:   Rest.
Day 5:   1 mile easy jogging, or some other sport.
Day 6:   Rest.
Day 7:   Warm up over $\frac{1}{2}$ mile, then do a fast 10 minutes running.

The summer schedule: week 6

Day 1:   Rest.
Day 2:   2 miles of fast-and-slow training, but with the fast bursts lasting $\frac{1}{4}$ mile, with a correspondingly longer jog.
Day 3:   Rest.
Day 4:   2 miles of fast-and-slow training, with the fast bursts of 100 to 200 yards.

Days 5
and 6:   Rest.
Day 7:   ½-mile warm-up. Time trial over 1 or 1½ miles.

Comments on the summer schedule

None of these sessions is very long. The hardest will take no more than 20 minutes, but you are using your body and in particular your legs much more intensively than in the past. You are also trying to improve your best times over short distances, and this too will put more strain on your system. It is therefore more important than usual to have the hard sessions spaced out, with a rest day or an easy day after each one. You may feel a bit stiff the next day, but a day of normal walking and stretching should leave you feeling good, even enthusiastic, about the next session.

Timing and distances

When you are running these short distances, accurate times obviously become more important. If you have a regular course near you, you will be able to judge your improvement, even if the distance is not known. Alternatively, you can find a running track – most schools have a grass track marked out in the summer. For timing, a wristwatch with a second hand is perfectly sufficient.

You can work out a 1-mile course fairly accurately by pacing the distance around the boundary of a cricket pitch, park, or piece of beach. With a normal stride of 1 yard, pace out a circuit of 300, 400 or 500 yards approximately, then work out how many laps you need for the 1760 yards. You probably won't be more than 20 yards a lap out, and that is only going to mean plus or minus 15 seconds at the most. It does give you the encouragement of seeing your improvement. (See also 'Measuring Distances' p. 38.)

The autumn schedule

When to use it:

When you want to increase your stamina.

When the weather is pleasant but not too hot.

When you have the time and the inclination to spend a bit longer on your training.

After the basic schedule week 8, or after the summer, spring or winter schedules.

Long term goals:

To run 6 miles in 60 minutes.

To run 4 miles in 34 minutes.

This part of the schedule is necessarily longer in mileage than any of the others, but not very intensive. If you have learned to like running, you will know that nothing gives you greater pleasure than to run on a calm autumn day, just ticking off the miles without feeling uncomfortable. Fortunately runners have discovered that you can improve your time over long distances by training over short distances. If you do the long run at weekends, the training during the week need not be a lot longer than usual.

The autumn schedule: week 1

Objective: To run 12 miles during the week.

Day 1:   3 miles at a steady speed, or 30 minutes.

Day 2:   Rest.

Day 3:   Another 3 miles, on a different course. Try 15 minutes out, going steadily, then pushing a bit harder on the way home.

Day 4:   Rest.

Day 5:   2 miles of fast-and-slow running, as previously described.

Day 6:   Rest.

Day 7:   4 miles, or 45 minutes, of slow, steady jogging.

The autumn schedule: week 2

Objective: To run 15 miles in the week.
Day 1: A 4-mile or 40-minute steady jog.
Day 2: Rest.
Day 3: 2 or 3 miles of fast-and-slow training. The faster
stretches should be 400 to 600 yards long, and the
slow jogging patches 200 to 300 yards .
Day 4: Rest.
Day 5: A 3-mile brisk run going as fast as is comfortable.
Day 6: Rest.
Day 7: 6 miles of slow jogging, trying to keep running most
of the way. Complete the distance, even if you have to
walk some of the last part of it.

The autumn schedule: week 3

Objective: To run 6 miles in 63 minutes.
Repeat week 2, in order to get used to the increased mileage.
Make sure that your footwear is comfortable and giving adequate
protection. You may need more cushioning if you run on roads.
Time yourself over the 6-mile run and aim for 63 minutes.

The autumn schedule: week 4

Objective: To run 4 miles in 36 minutes.
Day 1: 40 minutes steady jogging.
Day 2: Rest.
Day 3: 3 miles of fast-and-slow training, as before.
Day 4: Rest.
Day 5: 2 miles at a brisk pace.
Day 6: Rest.
Day 7: A trial over 4 miles aiming at 36 minutes. This is only
9 minutes per mile, and by now your stamina will have
increased enough to maintain this speed.

The autumn schedule: week 5

Objective: 5 miles in 48 minutes.
Day 1:   45 minutes of slow jogging, which is about 4 miles.
Day 2:   Rest.
Day 3:   Briskly run round a 3-mile course taking about 25 minutes.
Day 4:   Rest.
Day 5:   3 miles of fast-and-slow training, as before.
Day 6:   Rest.
Day 7:   A 5-mile course at a slower speed than last week, so you should have a bit in hand for the last mile. The rate is 9½ minutes per mile.

The autumn schedule: week 6

Objectives: 4 miles in 34 minutes.
            6 miles in 60 minutes.
Day 1:   3 miles at a steady pace, without pushing yourself.
Day 2:   Rest.
Day 3:   A 6-mile run. The required pace is 10 minutes a mile, so pick out a nice scenic route, not too hilly, and just keep chugging along.
Day 4:   Rest.
Day 5:   2 or 3 miles at a steady pace, with a few easy periods of striding out. Don't push yourself.
Day 6:   Rest.
Day 7:   The 4-mile trial. The speed here is faster, but having run 6 miles, 4 miles should seem easy so you can afford to go off quite quickly.

Comments on the autumn schedule

The emphasis here is on stamina rather than speed. It is therefore important that you find somewhere nice to run, otherwise you are going to get bored stiff. Doing the relatively fast times for the 4-mile course is less important than getting used to the increased mileage. If you have any problems, keep to 15 miles a week, but take it more slowly. This increased stamina will do you a lot of good when you come round to tackling the spring schedule again.

What next?

If you have got through the basic schedule, and have gone through the spring, summer and autumn schedules, you may have the ambition to go still further. If you have done all of these sessions, you can count yourself as really fit by jogging standards, but of course you are a long way from becoming a real runner. There is no such thing as total fitness – there is always a fresh challenge. As you get older you may find it sufficiently challenging to keep up the schedules in this book. As a comparison with runners, look at the table *One hundred steps to super-fitness*. The highest level reached in these schedules is step 39, so that leaves you with plenty of room for improvement. If you have been bitten by the running bug and want to take it more seriously, try the schedule in my earlier book *Naturally Fit* or join a running club.

One hundred steps to super-fitness

Step	Distance (miles)	Time (minutes)	
1	walk 1	20	
2	walk 1	18	
3	walk 1	15	
4	walk 2	40	
5	walk 2	35	
6	walk-trot 1	12	
7	walk 2	30	
8	walk-trot 1	10	
9	walk 3	45	
10	walk-trot $1\frac{1}{2}$	18	
11	walk-trot $1\frac{1}{2}$	16	
12	walk 4	60	
13	trot-walk $1\frac{1}{2}$	15	
14	trot $1\frac{1}{2}$	14	
15	walk-trot 4	55	
16	trot-walk 2	22	
17	trot-walk 2	20	
18	walk-trot 4	50	[steps 19–100 overleaf]

Step	Distance (miles)	Time (minutes)
19	trot 2	19
20	trot 1½	13
21	trot-walk 4	45
22	trot 1½	12
23	trot 3	32
24	trot 2	18
25	walk-trot 5	60
26	trot 2	17
27	trot 2	16
28	trot 3	30
29	trot-walk 4	42
30	trot 2½	20
31	trot 3	27
32	trot 3	25
33	trot 4	39
34	trot 3	24
35	trot 5	50
36	trot 3	23
37	trot 2	15
38	trot 3	22
39	trot 4	35
40	trot 4	33
41	run 2	14
42	run 4	31
43	trot 5	45
44	run 3	21
45	run 4	30
46	run 4	29
47	run 5	40
48	run 4	28
49	run 5	38
50	run 3	20
51	run 5	36
52	run 5	35
53	trot 6	45
54	run 4	27
55	run 5	34

Step	Distance (miles)	Time (minutes)
56	run 3	19
57	run 4	26
58	run 5	33
59	run 6	44
60	run 6	43
61	run 6	42
62	run 4	25
63	run 6	41
64	run 6	40
65	run 5	32
66	trot 8	60
67	run 6	39
68	run 7	49
69	run 6	38
70	run 7	48
71	run 3	18
72	run 7	47
73	run 7	46
74	run 6	37
75	run 10	75
76	run 7	45
77	run 7	44
78	run 8	54
79	run 8	53
80	run 4	24
81	run 8	52
82	run 8	51
83	run 5	30
84	run 9	60
85	run 10	70
86	run 9	59
87	run 8	50
88	run 9	58
89	run 6	36
90	run 9	57
91	run 10	65
92	run 9	56

Step	Distance (miles)	Time (minutes)
93	run $9\frac{1}{2}$	60
94	run 8	48
95	run 9	55
96	run 5	29
97	run 9	54
98	run 6	35
99	run 9	53
100	run 10	60

7 The jogger's problems

The biggest problem: feeling foolish

Apart from inertia, the main thing which stops people from going out jogging is the fear of looking silly. This applies particularly to those who are overweight and need the exercise most of all. A friend of mine started a jogging group in his road. At first, it comprised just a couple of his friends and their children. Then they persuaded their wives to join them. One of them was really seriously overweight, and had for years been too embarrassed to take part in any kind of sport. After a few weeks of jogging in the winter evenings and of watching her diet, she started to lose weight significantly. The more she lost weight, the more she felt like taking exercise, and, of course, the more she took exercise the slimmer she became. Now she plays tennis, runs, goes out, and enjoys life a lot more.

In organizing a group the first thing to do is to read over the reasons for jogging. Why should you do it? Are you convinced you are right? Good. You're convinced you are right and I am convinced too. The next thing to do is to convince one other person, at least, and get them to agree to join you. Now you have companionship as well as a sense of rectitude. The third thing is to pick a time, and place where you can jog undisturbed – like a quiet housing estate. I can guarantee that if you can keep it going for four weeks you'll be so proud of yourself that you'll jog anywhere, and you'll soon be jogging down your main shopping street on a Saturday morning. Remember: you are right. You are doing the right thing, and the kind of people who make remarks are only envious of your willpower.

Jogging in the city: the safety factor

As far as possible, jog in traffic-free areas – parks, playing fields, and so on. The local school, if asked nicely, would make a good centre for a jogging group. If you have to jog in the town, go for the back roads, and stick to places where the pavements are wide. If you are forced to run on main roads without pavements, keep to the edge of the road and run facing the traffic. I have often been forced to run on main roads. I used main roads for 3,000 miles across America – and in 40,000 miles of running I have never been in an accident, caused an accident or even heard of an accident caused by a jogger. I find that when I am running, my senses are particularly sharp. I use my ears as well as my eyes in order to be aware of traffic.

If, in Great Britain, you run on the right hand side of the road, then all you have to beware of is traffic coming from a road or gateway on your right. As long as you approach road junctions with caution, you won't have any trouble. Use these places as chances to slow down and get your breath back. Don't run across a road in your time trials – the enthusiasm to run fast can blunt your awareness of traffic.

Pavements can be a problem, if you have to cross several road junctions. If the traffic is very light, I run in the gutter to avoid hopping on and off pavements, because that can be very hard on the heels and the calf muscles. If you have to go up and down pavements, take it gently, and be sure to have good shoes.

Having said all that, lots of people do jog safely in towns. When I lived in London I used to jog from Hampstead to the City every morning – it was just as quick as public transport, more reliable and a lot cheaper.

Jogging in the country

It is a lot easier to jog in the country, where there is less traffic, less pollution, and where there are fewer people. But it has its problems too. The city is quite anonymous. The jogger in the country village does attract attention, and it is less easy to find a track or a park. However, most villages have a football field and a cricket field, and these make ideal jogging places. If you are some way out of the village you are faced with a choice between narrow country lanes, with cars whizzing round blind corners, or going into the open fields, where there are growing crops, nettles, cattle, barbed wire and electric fences. The solution to this is to jog on the footpaths. These are often signposted, but the best thing is to use the local ordnance survey one inch or 1:50,000 map. This will show all the paths where you have a right of way. From this you can work out circuits of different distances.

Good places to run in the country are: footpaths, bridle paths, river or canal banks, firebreaks in forest land, and hayfields or cornfields after harvest.

Places you should avoid in the country are: fields with growing crops, newly-sown fields, and fields with stock in them. However, it is usually possible to go through gates and round the edges of fields without causing any harm to anyone.

Country people like their privacy, like anyone else, and if the track you are jogging along leads into a farm, you may find yourself face to face with the farmer. If you smile, apologize, and treat him like a human being, he will do the same for you, and probably tell you a good way to get home.

Occasionally you come across a landowner who would like to prosecute every trespasser. Keep your cool. For a start, he cannot prosecute you unless you have caused damage. He is entitled to ask you to leave his property, which you should do. If he is rude, smile and thank him – it will infuriate him.

Dogs, cattle and other animals

Dogs like chasing things, and they may chase you. It is little comfort when you are leapt upon by 100lb of bull mastiff to be told 'he's only playing' by the owner; by that time you are flat on your back and scared stiff. Dogs on leads should be given a wide berth, in case they suddenly dart out and trip you. If you are chased by a loose dog, stand still and it will lose interest.

At worst, it will mistake you for a tree. As you become faster and more experienced, you can challenge less fit dogs such as middle-aged corgis and dachshunds. If you increase speed gradually they will pursue you, yapping, until they collapse exhausted. This gives you some fun and the dog some exercise.

Cattle can be terrifying to the city-dweller. Heifers and young steers are very curious, and will gallop after anything strange. If you turn round and wave your arms at them they will shy away. Wild bulls on the loose are a very unusual sight, but if you see a single large bovine creature in a field, check on its gender before going near its path.

Animals are a danger only when they are startled, frightened, defending their young or their territory. This is true of lions, buffalo, rattlesnakes, elephants, bears, hyenas, adders and coyotes, all of which I have encountered in my time. Make sure they know you are coming and if there is a confrontation, don't be proud or aggressive; retreat in an organized manner and keep your eye on them.

What surface is best to run on ?

My first rule is that the ground should be fairly even; otherwise you'll fall over, twist an ankle, and do yourself more harm than good. The ideal surface is firm but not rock hard, with enough give in it to prevent you jarring your feet, but not so soft that it holds you back. British grass is ideal, thanks to year-round rainfall, and so are firm sand and the trails in the pinewoods of Scandinavia and North America. Soft sand and ploughed fields are used by some athletes, but they are far from ideal for the jogger: they are picked because they are so difficult to run on. Some countries make jogging trails around the parks by covering the hard ground with sawdust or wood shavings and this makes a very nice surface.

Paths made of dirt or cinders are slightly better than roads because they jar the feet less. However, there is nothing wrong with roads for jogging on as long as you have the right shoes. I try to alternate between roads and grass. Tarmac is good for time trial courses because it is a reliable surface in wet weather.

You can run on snow up to about a foot deep, then you have to stick to beaten trails. If it becomes packed and icy you will need studded shoes. I know a man who ran a 500-mile race in snowshoes, so don't be discouraged.

Hills: are they good for you?

When you start to jog do so on flat or nearly flat ground. It is quite hard enough getting started without making it more difficult. I suggest you don't tackle hills at all for the first two weeks. When you do, start by taking them very gently, both up and down, because they impose different strains on your legs. Walking in the hills is a very good way of toughening up your muscles, so walk before you jog.

When you are getting fitter – say after four weeks – and have adjusted your jogging pace to going up and down slopes, then you can start incorporating hills in your training. One of the sayings of Arthur Lydiard, the great New Zealand coach, is 'The hills will find you out.' Running up hills makes you work much harder, and puts a much greater strain on your cardio-vascular system. When you are getting fit, running in the hills will make you a lot fitter, but you must build up to them gradually. Don't go and start your jogging programme by running straight up your nearest hill, just because Peter Snell used to do it. When I am coaching runners we normally do one session per week for running up and down a hill, but not until we have at least four weeks of running 20 miles a week behind us.

Jogging at night

Unless you are very lucky and have a lot of time to spare, you are sometimes going to be faced with the prospect of going out jogging in the dark, or else not jogging at all. Pick a route you have already used in daylight, so that you know what is coming. City streets and many recreation areas have enough street lighting for you to be able to run quite safely, but if there is traffic, wear white clothing, or put strips of reflecting tape on to your tracksuit. If you are in the country, where there is no lighting, carry a small hand torch so that you can be seen by traffic.

You do need to be certain of the ground you are running on, so that you don't stumble or trip. For this reason, the road is the best surface for running on at night. It is very seldom completely dark when you go out jogging. If the visibility really is zero, due to a combination of darkness and fog or rain, and the ground is unfamiliar, then stay at home and try some indoor exercise.

Jogging and business life

There was a time not so long ago, when large business lunches and expense-account evenings out were considered prime incentives for a young executive. Things are changing. We are now aware of the effects of over-indulgence, the link between cholesterol and heart attacks, the links between smoking and lung cancer. More and more businessmen realize that if they are to remain effective, or even alive, they have to look after themselves. There is still a reluctance to lead the way. Just as schoolboys know that they really ought to work for their exams but look down on the swot, many of us take pride in our physical condition but are shy of doing anything about it. Fortunately there are now examples of leading figures who are not afraid to be seen jogging. The Americans lead the way, of course. Central Park in New York is never without joggers in daylight hours, and the paths get quite congested at peak jogging times. The same is true of the beaches of Santa Monica and the fields of UCLA. In Great Britain public figures make time for jogging: Roy Hattersley sees it as the only way of surviving the pressures of being an M.P. Jan Hildreth, Director of Great Britain's Institute of Directors, runs daily, and is a constant preacher of the virtues of running as a means of maintaining both bodily health and mental equilibrium.

The constant complaint is 'I haven't time'. If you spend an

hour a week jogging, that is 50 hours a year, 1,000 hours in 20 years, but in exchange for those 40 days you increase your life expectancy by years (see the section on jogging and longevity in Chapter 8). You must make time. If you are making a timetable for a conference, it is easy enough to put in '7.30 am jogging (optional)', or put it in before lunch, or before dinner. Get a colleague to agree to come with you, and you will be surprised how many others will join, once they have a leader.

Fitting jogging into the daily routine is also easier if you have some companions. The first 20 minutes of the lunch hour is the best time – all you miss is an extra drink. Once you have established that you are going out jogging at a specific time, it is amazing how keen other people will be to keep you up to the mark. Unfortunately, for them, jogging is not like prayer: the effects are not transferable, you have to do it yourself to reap the benefits!

Jogging and social life

Is the jogger anti-social? Sometimes, yes. If my wife says 'Chris and Patsy want us to go for a drink at 12 o'clock', I am quite likely to go for my run at 11.45 and get to the party at 12.30. On the other hand, I reckon I can afford to drink more and go to more parties, with fewer after-effects, because I run. I love eating and drinking and dancing and meeting people. That's what I keep fit for.

If you get into the routine of running regularly, your body becomes better at regulating itself. It will soon tell you if you are over-indulging. If you dance a lot, you can count this as part of your week's training – I find that an hour in a disco is as strenuous as a four-mile run.

One effect of running regularly will be to cut down or abolish your cigarette smoking, and another will be that, being more thirsty, you will probably drink more beer and long drinks and fewer shorts, so that your total alcohol intake will go down. But you won't enjoy life any the less: quite the reverse, you will enjoy your social life more, and keep it up longer.

How to keep fit when you really have no time to spare

There are times when you can't get up early to jog because you need the sleep, you have important company all through the working day, followed by a long journey home and a busy evening. If it is only one or two days a week you can get your run on the other days, but what happens if you have to go for a couple of weeks like that? Here are a few ideas.

1 Cut your calorie intake slightly. If you are missing the daily jog, cut your food intake by 200–300 calories – the equivalent of tea and cake, or one helping of potatoes. This will prevent you putting on weight.
2 While sitting in your car or at your desk, take the occasional chance of stretching your legs and spine (see the section on staying flexible in Chapter 8). Practise a few seconds of isometric exercises on each muscle group in turn. This will help maintain muscle strength and your appearance.
3 Run everywhere, or walk fast. Even when crossing the yard, you can break into a couple of fast running strides. This has the effect of maintaining the muscles you use in running. Run upstairs in the house and, if you are in an office block, run up and down the stairs instead of using the lift. If you have to take someone important out to lunch, suggest a restaurant a few hundred yards away, and walk there and back. It may be, of course, that the important person jogs too, and you will get on a lot better for sharing a common interest.

The combination of all these efforts won't make you any fitter, but you won't lose your fitness nearly as quickly, and you will get back into running much more easily afterwards.

Jogging on holiday

This is probably the best opportunity of all for jogging because you have more time and new places to explore. There is no better way to get to know your new surroundings than by going out and jogging around. You can trot around, find the

94

attractive places and go back to them later. You don't have to be afraid of looking silly, because no one knows who you are.

A word of caution: don't get carried away and overdo it in the first two days. You have to adjust to several changes, so don't allow yourself to become exhausted. You may also find yourself running on a different surface, and you don't want to spoil your holiday by getting a sprained ankle.

You will probably be taking a holiday from your time trials as well because you won't have the same courses to time yourself over, but it is the effort that counts, so carry on with the schedule in the same form. If there is a running track near you, you can use that. Then you will be able to make direct comparisons, allowing for climatic factors.

You might meet other joggers, some on holiday and some local, and thereby you get a lot more out of the trip. I have struck up a lot of interesting friendships that way.

Jogging for travellers

Travelling is tiring. You arrive at your destination worn out. This is mostly mental tiredness, caused by anxiety and by the abrasion of the constant change and having to cope with new information. The best time to jog is soon after you arrive. Put your bags in your room, change into your running gear and trot gently around the neighbourhood. The physical effort need not be great. The mental relaxation you will get from it is terrific. I find that running in a new place helps me to feel at home. I find my way about, get my bearings, and get the tension out of my muscles. More important, I reassert my individuality. In a place where no one knows me, and where I have no place in the scheme of things, I re-establish continuity with the rest of my life, with the days of jogging at home, and with the runs that lie ahead. Having had my run, I am more sure of myself.

Time-changes and jet-lag

The effect of air travel is to give you a jaded feeling. Your stomach feels bloated from eating all that cotton-wool food, your feet and legs are swollen, your senses have been both over-stimulated and bored. You are tired, but you can't sleep. I have found that getting out and taking exercise is the quickest way to get back to normal. Your body has been kept in a state of suspended animation for hours and hours. It has almost certainly been over-fed. If you go for a gentle run it will burn up some of the calories, get your digestive system working properly and generally make you feel more like a human being and less like a captive balloon.

The upset to your natural rhythm caused by time-changes will take a few days to cure. West to East flights are more difficult to get over than east to west. If you get into the habit of taking exercise immediately after a journey, you will 'programme' your body to the new timing. You will get back into the routine of 'run, shower, eat, sleep', and being physically tired and mentally relaxed by the jogging, you will find that your sleep pattern is restored quite quickly. However, you should not expect to achieve the same running times as before your journey until the third day after arrival at the earliest, and the fifth day after arrival for a West-East flight. You must expect to find it more of an effort to run for the first couple of days. It is remarkable how quickly top-class sportsmen can adjust to time-changes. They can do this because their bodies are accustomed to regular physical work, and respond to that rather than to the 'internal clock'. Going out and exercising is equivalent to putting the clock right.

Altitude

As you get higher, there is less oxygen about, therefore your heart has to beat faster to get the same amount of oxygen into your muscles. If you step out of an aeroplane at an altitude of 8000 feet, you will notice that your pulse rate is considerably increased while you are just standing still, and goes up more

12 *A round-the-lake course has the advantage that you cannot cut the corners — and the pleasing view makes the exercise more soothing. (Topix)*

13 *Talking while you run is a good way of making sure you don't run too fast too soon. Looking where you are going is also a good idea. (Topix)*

14 *Lancaster University: the grounds of most schools and colleges are suitable for jogging. Note the man on the left: his head and body posture is perfect. (University of Lancaster)*

15 *This work-based group is a good advertisement for the sport. (Topix)*

16 *This is the lot of most of us — jogging alone in city streets. But it can be done if you choose your route — and your running shoes — with care. You will also get to know your neighbourhood better. (Topix)*

17 *Running with a club encourages you to stick to a regular routine: the results are worth the slight loss of independence. (Stone Jogging Club — Women's Section)*

18 *Members of the Stone Jogging Club after a taxing run — note the professional outfits and the appropriate shoes. (Topix)*

19 *Social activities and special events reinforce the philosophy of the Stone Jogging Club. This particular event is always part of the après-jog routine. (Topix)*

20 *Once you are really fit, you can try yourself out by running a fast mile on the track, like these* Sunday Times *writers: (left to right) John Lovesey, Norman Harris, and Cliff Temple. (Topix)*

21 *(Above) Fun runs form the natural climax of a jogging programme, giving people a chance to measure themselves by some standard. (Topix)*

22 *(Facing page) The longest jog of all: the author halfway through his 3000-mile trot from Los Angeles to New York. He averaged 45 miles a day. (Bruce Tulloh)*

23 *(Below) 2000 miles from Los Angeles and 1000 miles to New York: the author in St Louis. (Bruce Tulloh)*

24 *The author and his family completing the course at the Pepsi Fun Run in Southampton, 1978* (*Courtesy of Schweppes Ltd*)

25 *The start of the 1978* Sunday Times *National Fun Run Mass Jog in Hyde Park, London* (*Times Newspapers Ltd*)

when you walk about. If you immediately started running, your pulse rate might reach a dangerously high level.

Over a period of several weeks, your body responds to the altitude. The amount of haemoglobin in your blood goes up, so that you extract more oxygen from the atmosphere.

The rate at which you adjust depends on the altitude. Above 4000 feet you have to take it into account. It is quite simple – you go on perceived effort rather than speed. If your usual pace seems very hard, slow down until your breathing becomes comfortable. Use your heart rate as a guide and don't go above the safe upper limit. People adjust at considerably different rates, but usually the trained person adapts more quickly to altitude than the untrained. At such as around 5000 or 6000 feet, for example in Nairobi, you should be completely adjusted after two weeks, but at the 7500 feet level of Mexico City, three to four weeks is needed. Be particularly careful when you get over 10,000 feet, and don't think about jogging until you can walk quickly without discomfort.

Jogging in cold climates

This is really not much of a problem, because you can always put on more clothing. I start with singlet and Y-fronts, running shorts and T-shirt, then a cotton and nylon mixture tracksuit which is fleecy on the inside and wind-resistant on the outside. If the tracksuit has a hooded top, that is all you need to cope with a British winter.

It is important to keep your head warm in sub-zero conditions, and many runners wear woolly hats. The only additions needed in really cold conditions are mittens and a wind-and-waterproof anorak or cagoule. This should be light in weight, so that as you get warmer you can take it off and carry it.

Tracksuits should not be too close-fitting – they may look better but they won't keep you as warm as loose-fitting ones.

For running in cold weather you will need training shoes which are large enough for you to wear thick woollen socks inside. Thick snow presents the problem of keeping your feet dry. If you live in snowy conditions you will probably be cross-country skiing anyway, and there is no better fitness training than that. If it is just a matter of getting out in a bad week, I suggest you wear boots, with gaiters, or those flexible Wellington boots with studded soles, 'racing wellies'.

It is possible to jog in almost all conditions, so don't be put off when it goes down to near freezing, just make sure you are properly equipped.

Jogging in hot climates

The natural tendency for someone used to a cold climate is to strip off as soon as he gets some sunshine. This can be a bad mistake. If the sun is really strong you must protect yourself from sunburn. In extreme heat, over 95°F (35°C), you should wear Arab-style clothing – light cloaks or trousers, which will cut off the radiant heat from the sun, but allow sweat to evaporate.

In ordinary hot weather, between 70°F and 90°F, your only problems will be discomfort and dehydration. You cannot expect to run long distances as effectively in hot weather, and as your body temperature goes up you will tend to slow down. When it is really hot, keep the run short – not more than 20 minutes – and have a swim or a cold shower afterwards.

You will naturally sweat a lot, and this fluid should be replaced as soon as possible. The best argument for running in hot weather is the amount of cold beer you can drink afterwards. There are several drinks which replace the salts as well as the water, but special drinks are not essential. As long as you drink a lot in hot weather, you can make up the salt loss by taking extra salt with your meals. It is only the marathon runner or the long distance cyclist who needs specialist products. The ordinary person can rely on common sense and thirst to solve the problem.

The thing to be careful of is raising your body temperature too much. Don't lie in the sun for an hour and then go for a run. Start off cool – either by running in the early morning or by having a swim first – and cool off afterwards.

Jogging and other sports

A lot of people say, 'I don't need to jog, I play tennis regularly.' If you could check up on them, you might find that they play once or twice in May, once a week in June, once or twice a week in July and August and occasionally in September. They then have six months of doing very little, except when stricken by a guilty conscience and they go out and do two or three hours walking or gardening and then feel dreadfully stiff after it.

Jogging should not stop you doing all the other things you enjoy, it should make you more able to do them. If you keep your jogging programme going all the year round, you can take up almost any other sport without suffering the agonies of stiffness the next day.

The sports which do you the most good are the ones which exercise lots of different muscles, and the ones which keep you going continuously, thus strengthening your heart. Hence swimming, cycling, orienteering, beagling, cross-country skiing and rowing are all excellent. You have to balance the danger against the fun and benefits. Contact sports like rugby are highly energetic, but carry considerable risks. So does squash, although it is very good for giving you exercise in a short space of time. What I have against squash is that it is fiercely competitive, and the level of exercise is not always safely controlled. Most people are sensible but I have seen middle-aged men work themselves into a state of total collapse rather than allow themselves to be beaten by a younger man.

If you do a sport you enjoy, fit it into your jogging plan. If it isn't fast enough to make you sweat, it is probably not doing you much good physically.

Jogging around the world

I have managed to run in about forty different countries so far, but it isn't always easy in places where they are not used to joggers. One advantage you have is that you are moving quite fast, and by the time people have got over their astonishment you have passed by.

The most serious obstacles are official and officious people, the kind who assume that everything which is not compulsory is forbidden. I was once told off for running along a footpath, by a forestry official. When I replied that footpaths were meant for feet, he said 'only for walking, not running'. In some cities in the USA anyone on foot in the street is automatically regarded with suspicion, because this implies that he is too poor to own a car.

Northern Europe is a good place for joggers, particularly Scandinavia and Germany where the virtues of good health are appreciated. In southern Europe they will merely laugh at you, but in less developed parts of the world people may set their dogs after you, which is nasty. In most countries of the world children will run after you, but in Kenya they overtake you, which is disconcerting.

You must realize that a running figure in some countries is an unusual sight, so don't go dashing through narrow streets or native bazaars, and steer clear of official property such as army barracks. The best thing to do, if you don't speak the language, is to find a small circuit in an uncrowded area and keep going round it. This will demonstrate that you are merely taking exercise and therefore are a crazy rather than a dangerous foreigner. Luckily, running is a worldwide sport, and you will find athletics federations and running clubs everywhere if you want to run seriously.

The jogger's repartee

Talking to your companion while you are running is a good thing. It helps to make the miles pass and it keeps you from running too fast. If you get fed up with your companion's conversation you can always speed up a little bit.

However, what do you say to the chap who shouts rude things at you as you run down the street? In general, a dignified silence is best, and it saves your breath. The kind of people who shout at you in the street are suffering from a feeling of inferiority because you are jogging and they are not. They are trying to restore their self-esteem by forcing you to notice them, so ignoring them and their rude remarks is the right reaction.

If the remark is made in a foreign language, and you don't know whether it is rude or not, a smile and a condescending wave is the ideal answer. If the remark is so obviously insulting that you want to answer back, be sure that you are fit enough to outrun the other guy. I was once taking a group of boys on a run and we passed a building site. One of the building workers shouted something offensive and the smallest boy yelled back: 'Belt up, or I'll 'ang one on yer!' Other suitable all-purpose phrases are 'You too, mate!' (Great Britain), 'Up yer flue, blue!' (Australia) and 'Same to you, fella!' (USA). Delivered with sufficient aggression they should put the shouter off from shouting at the next jogger who passes that way.

If you are short of breath you can use gestures – one finger raised and wagged indicates that you do not approve of his behaviour. Two fingers raised indicates, of course, that you will have two miles left to run. A useful all-purpose gesture, indicating power, a sportsmanlike attitude and sympathy with the working classes, is to raise the right forearm, with a clenched fist, and give it a vigorous upward thrust. In socialist countries, of course, the left arm should be raised.

8 The jogger's health

Jogging and longevity

If you want to live longer, there is no better way of increasing your expectation of life than by a graduated exercise programme. One can always find the odd example of the old man who has lived to a ripe old age while smoking heavily, drinking gin and never walking a step if he can help it, but statistics tell the true story. Since Professor J. N. Morris's famous study on London 20 years ago, more and more studies have shown that people who take exercise in their middle years outlive those who do not. Physical exercise in working hours helps, but it seems to be exercise during leisure hours which is the best pointer.

In 1973 the Medical Research Council's Social Medicine Unit, with Professor Morris at the head, published the results of a four-year study on health and exercise in middle-aged civil servants. The life patterns of those who had had heart attacks were compared with computer-matched controls. The men were classified into those who took regular energetic exercise and those who did not. Over a four-year period, of the 134 in the group which took exercise, only 23 (17.1 per cent) had heart attacks, while in the sedentary group, in which there were 508 people, 191 (37.6 per cent) had heart attacks. Even though the type of exercise was not scientifically controlled, the message is very clear.

Studies on the effects on middle-aged men of controlled exercise, by Fred Kasch in San Diego and the Medical Research Council in London, show the same thing: those who exercised stayed younger than those who did not.

So, if you want to live out all the years you have been given, the message is clear – get moving! But be careful. You cannot impose new stresses on the body too suddenly. Parts of you, particularly your feet and legs, are going to have to work harder than they have done for several years, and they may react against it.

Through running you will become your own doctor. You will learn about your own body, and learn to pick out slight ups and downs in your health which would escape the less alert. Before you reach this state of knowledge, though, there will be a time when you suffer strange aches and pains, and times when you feel just below par. Should you run at these times or not? If you do run what precautions should you take? I hope that most of the precautions are built in to my schedules but everybody reacts in different ways.

The guiding principle: maintaining equilibrium

We run to get healthy and to stay healthy. The guiding principle should be to maintain your state of health, or to improve it gradually. When you consider a training session, the question is: 'Is this going to build me up or run me down?' If you never did anything that caused you even mild discomfort, you would never take enough exercise to do you any good. On the other hand, if you were to go out for a run determined to push yourself to your utmost physical limits, and the next day you do the same again, and the same the day after, you would break down within a week. What I have learned, in over 30 years running, is how much to do at any one time. I have also learned that individuals differ enormously and that one cannot prescribe the same dose for all 16-year-old schoolboys, or for all 40-year-old women.

The ideal condition when you are training is that you are running moderately fast, breathing more deeply and more frequently than usual, but not getting out of breath. You are feeling a warm glow all over, maybe even sweating a bit, but you are not uncomfortably hot. Your stride is even, economical of effort (which means not too long) and your body is balanced but not tense. Your heart is beating at something between

120 and 150 beats a minute, your brain is clear and your senses are alert. You can think and you can talk. One school of thought holds that you should never run so fast that you cannot carry on a conversation at the same time. I think that this holds good for most of the training, but when doing the time trials you will get a bit more out of breath.

When you have finished your run you will get your breathing back to normal almost immediately, but you will feel a little tired. After having a shower and changing you will feel slightly tired in body, but refreshed in mind. You will be able to get on with the things you have to do with a feeling of physical satisfaction. The following day you should feel completely recovered. Any slight stiffness will disappear during the first few minutes after you get out of bed. You will be looking forward to the next run. In other words, your body is in a state of healthy equilibrium. It can cope with the training load you put on it, and it responds by getting stronger.

This is the ideal. But how do we cope when things do not go smoothly?

Tiredness

This is the jogger's greatest enemy. How do you know if it is real? Often the tiredness is mental, produced by overloading the mind. Sometimes it is caused by traffic fumes and the stresses of travelling. The only way to find out is to put your gear on and start a gentle jog. Tell yourself that you are going to take it very easily, and if you are too tired you can always stop. If the tiredness is mental, you will start to feel better within five minutes of gentle jogging. If it is real physical tiredness you will not be able to maintain your steady pace without becoming more tired. If that is the case, walk home and have a real rest – put your feet up for half an hour, and put off your training until the following day. The schedules demand training for only three or four days a week, and if you are lacking in sleep or tired from working it is better to get over that than to force yourself out running.

On feeling bad

Some days when you are running up a hill, or when you are nearing the end of your time trial course and have been a bit over-optimistic, you start to feel bad. Your legs feel heavier than usual, you get an uncomfortable feeling in the pit of your stomach, your head starts to get hot and your chest muscles feel tight. Your heart, if you have time to think about it, is going at about 170 or 180 beats a minute. Slow down, but don't panic. You are not about to die, you are merely experiencing what serious athletes go through several times a week – you are pushing yourself close to the limit. What would happen if you exceeded it? You might collapse, or faint for a moment. You can take it from me that you have not got anywhere near the limit yet – it is merely a warning, which joggers should heed. Only a fool or a very ambitious runner goes on pushing when these warning signs appear. If you ease to a gentle jog, or even walk, your pulse and breathing will get back to normal rates within three or four minutes. If you go out for a run the next day you may feel rather sluggish, but the day after that you should be fine.

Coughs and colds

The rule here is: if in doubt, don't go out. Minor virus infections often affect you when you are run down. If it is just a sniffle or a slight cough, I suggest you put on your track suit, including head covering, and go out for a 'jog as you please' session. This will raise your body temperature and may drive off the infection. If, however, you have an above-normal body temperature, a rapid pulse rate at rest, or are feeling hot and feverish, you should not attempt to jog at all. You should not attempt to train hard when you have any sort of general infection.

Influenza

In the British climate, we often get 'flu' epidemics of varying severity during the winter. It makes sense to get yourself vaccinated against flu as soon as the outbreak starts, but sometimes there are different strains of the virus about, so that vaccination does not give complete protection. Even if the virus is one of the 24-hour types, it should still be treated with respect. You should not go jogging until you have recovered and given yourself a couple of days of just walking. There have been one or two cases, within the last five years, of athletes going out and training or racing while still infected, with the result that the heart muscle itself became infected and the athlete died. This gives the sport a bad name, so please don't do it.

Asthma and hay fever

Some asthmatics avoid all exercise, others seem to have a compulsive drive towards it. In a high percentage of asthmatics, attacks occur after jogging, and treatment is needed. However, on the positive side, many of them find that their asthma is less severe and more easily controlled when they improve their personal fitness. A friend of mine, Martin Hyman, reached Olympic level as a long distance runner, in spite of suffering from asthma in the winter and hay fever in the summer. The latter complaint is uncomfortable, but should not stop you getting out. The message is, therefore, that you can train, but have your inhaler handy.

Minor injuries

Unless the injuries are to feet or legs, they should not stop you jogging completely. Better to jog gently, or walk, and maintain your general fitness, than to wallow in idleness. It just makes it harder to get started again afterwards. If you have strapping or plaster on, make sure that it does not become loose through running or chafe your skin.

Jogger's kidney

Occasionally athletic pseudonephritis or jogger's kidney is reported. This is the presence of protein in the urine, together with some blood, but unless the symptoms are severe and persistent they may be ignored.

Jock itch

This is a slightly embarassing and uncomfortable complaint affecting male runners. Chafing occurs in your crutch, caused by a jock strap or Y-fronts that are too tight. The treatment is a little ointment or vaseline to stop the rubbing. Sometimes a persistent itch may develop, which is due to a fungal infection similar to that causing athlete's foot. It should be treated with fungicide cream.

Jogger's nipple

This painful condition can affect both men and women. It is caused by chafing from a running vest or T-shirt which is too tight. The treatment is to rub a little vaseline on to the affected part, and the cure is to wear a looser vest next time. Bra-less running is not recommended for women – though men may enjoy it!

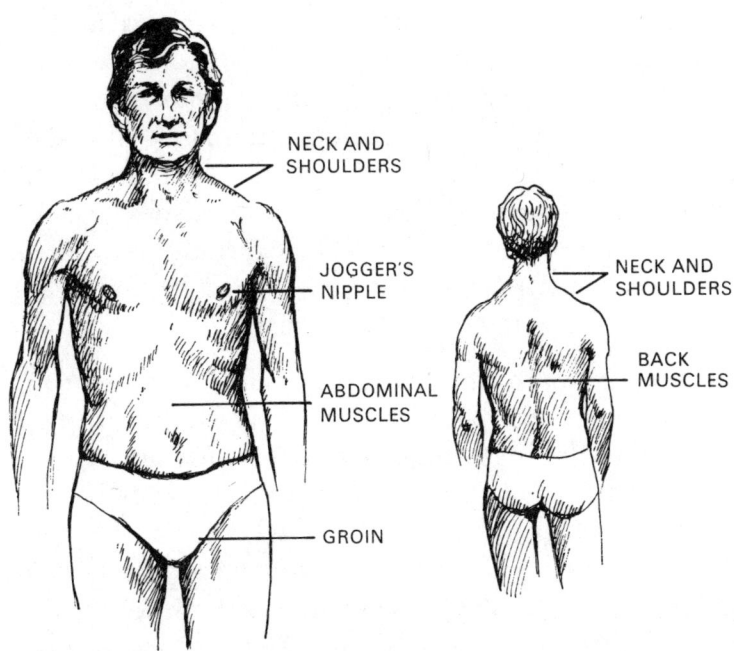

Danger points in the body

Back trouble

When you are jogging, your back and stomach muscles have to work to keep you upright. You can always tell when someone is really tired by the way they sag. If you start with too ambitious a programme, you may find your back muscles are stiff the next day. This applies particularly to overweight people, because the strain on the back muscles is that much greater. The answer to this is that your back muscles will get stronger with walking and jogging, and the stiffness can be eased by doing flexibility exercises. If you get serious and persistent back pain see your doctor.

Staying flexible

When you start jogging, or when you have had a particularly hard run, you will find yourself stiff the next day. This stiffness will be mostly in the legs, but you may also find that the muscles in the small of your back and your shoulders are stiff too. Slight stiffness is to be expected when you start – that is why the schedule has rest days in it, to allow your body to adjust. If you go on running when you are really stiff, your range of movements becomes very limited, and you shuffle along like an old man. The way to avoid this is to do a set of loosening and stretching exercises either before or after your day's jog. They should be done slowly, not jerkily, so that the muscles are stretched gradually. I have listed them, starting from the top of your body, so that it is easy to remember them.

1 Head rolling: just roll your head round and round slowly.
2 Arm rotating: swing both arms in complete circles, first one way and then the other, until they are swinging smoothly.
3 Trunk rotating: put your hands on your hips, bend your trunk forwards, and rotate it three times one way then three times the other, bending as far forwards and as far backwards as possible. Carry on until your muscles are loosened up.
4 Toe touching: stand with your feet about 18 inches apart. lean forwards with your arms hanging down, then press

your hands down towards the ground. Hold that position for two seconds, then relax, and then press again.

5 Calf stretching: stand with your feet together, then cross your right foot in front of the left. Clasp your hands together and push down towards your right foot. Try not to fall over! Push your hands down, relax, then cross your feet the other way round and repeat the exercise.

Is jogging enough?

As long as you combine it with flexibility exercises, yes, it is. It gives you heart training, muscular strength and endurance, weight control, confidence and mental relaxation. There are lots of other possible exercise programmes, based on the use of gymnasia, swimming baths, weight training rooms and so on, but jogging, or running, is the easiest, cheapest and most natural way to take the exercise that our bodies need.

On the other hand, the mere act of going for a jog is not a talisman that will protect you from all ills. I hope that in reading this book you have realized that jogging is a way of getting to understand your body, so that you learn to treat it in the right way. To take a crude example, if you habitually gorge yourself in the evenings, taking in say 500 calories more than you need, then jogging a mile a day will not stop you from putting on weight. You only burn up 100 calories a mile. In the same way, jogging will not stop you getting lung cancer if you are a heavy smoker, or stop you destroying your liver if you drink a lot. What does happen is that the person who commits himself to jogging becomes far more aware of his own health, and also acquires the self-discipline to control his self-destructive habits.

Smoking and drinking

Both of these are enjoyable social habits, and as the whole point of a fitness programme is to help you enjoy life more, I am not going to come straight out and say that the jogger should not smoke or drink. I really enjoy smoking a cigar after a good dinner, and I have no intention of giving up the habit. But I only smoke about one a week, so the harm caused, if any, is infinitesimal. What about one a day, you may ask, or two or three cigarettes a day? Where do we draw the line? We draw the line at the point where the body ceases to be able to cope with these poisons – which they are, even though they may be pleasant poisons.

It is really common sense to draw the line at anything above one cigar or four cigarettes a day, and even then I would suggest that you have one nicotine-free day a week to allow your system to clear. To test whether it is doing you any harm, try giving up for two weeks, or for Lent. If you feel healthier after giving up even a small intake, then they are probably doing you some harm, and it is up to you to make the decision.

Drink is a bit easier, because we know the rate at which a healthy liver can break down alcohol. So far no one has come out with anything against alcohol in moderation, and one can cope with a bottle of wine or four pints of beer a day without trouble. If you are running regularly, and working up a thirst, you can really enjoy your beer, especially as it is replacing both the fluid and the salts that you lost while running. You must remember that alcohol is rich in calories – reckon on about 100 calories per drink.

Jogging and your sex life

You may have seen car stickers with slogans like 'Runners make better lovers', and 'Marathon runners can keep it up for over two hours'. It is quite true. You may not be feeling very strong immediately after a hard run, but the general improvement in your health, combined with the fact that you will look better, feel better and weigh less, will probably improve your sexual vitality. The fact that your heart and your back muscles will be stronger through jogging will mean that sex itself will be less tiring and your recovery rate will be quicker. Jogging keeps you young.

Jogging in old age

I must, reluctantly, admit that none of us is immortal, but this does not mean we have to admit defeat. Men and women of over 90 swim, walk and run regularly, A man of 94 has run a marathon, and I recently climbed Snowdon with a very fit 90 year old. The jogger's **hero** is Larry Lewis, who went on running regularly up to his death at the age of 104.

When you get over 80 you may start having to make a few concessions, because your joints become less flexible and your bones more brittle as you get older. You must do your stretching exercises slowly and thoroughly every day. You will find that vigorous walking will get your heart rate up to its safe level of 130–140 beats per minute, and jogging should be confined to flat level ground, because of the greater risk of injury.

As long as you use common sense, and employ the experience you have gained in all those years, you can go on enjoying physical exercise all your life.

9 The jogger's feet and legs

Napoleon's army may have marched on its stomach, but its lack of boots didn't help. The jogger is only as good as his feet will allow him to be. The other side of the coin is that if you learn to look after your feet and legs, they will last you longer than those of the non-jogger. It often horrifies me to see people in their 50s or 60s and sometimes even in their 40s, who have let themselves get into such a state that they cannot walk half a mile without discomfort. These are the tarmac people. They can only function as long as they have a vehicle to carry them around and as a result they miss a lot of things in life. These are people who spend their summer holidays parked in lay-bys, because they cannot make the effort to walk over the hill and see what lies beyond.

For the jogger, to whom three or four miles on foot is a pleasure, not a pain, the country is full of barely explored, interesting places. The use of your feet gives you the freedom of the countryside, with its paths, ridgeways, hills and woods, so enjoy it.

Avoiding injuries

If you act sensibly, you should never get any serious injuries at all. In 20 years of running in races, I have never had to miss a single event through injury, and that is imposing far more strain than the jogger will encounter.

The most important thing is your running posture. You must be balanced, without any part of your body being held awkwardly. For the jogger, this means running in the most natural and easy way possible – not over-striding, not trying to copy someone else's running action, not pointing your toes inwards or outwards, and not trying to run on your toes. In particular, your shoes should allow your foot to spread out properly, so that the weight is distributed evenly, as described in the section 'How to jog' in Chapter 3.

Injuries are usually described by the parts they affect, as for example jogger's foot, or jogger's shin, although these terms may cover several different kinds of injury, some affecting muscles and tendons, and some affecting joints and the ligaments that bind them together. With the help of Dr John Davies, Sports Medicine Consultant at Guy's Hospital, London, I have listed all the troubles that may occur, and the recommended treatment for them.

Jogger's foot

Included in this term may be the following complaints:

Athlete's foot
This is an infectious fungus disease, spread by contact with changing-room floors, bath mats, towels and other moist surfaces. It is inconvenient rather than serious – you get cracks and soreness between the toes. It can easily be treated with a

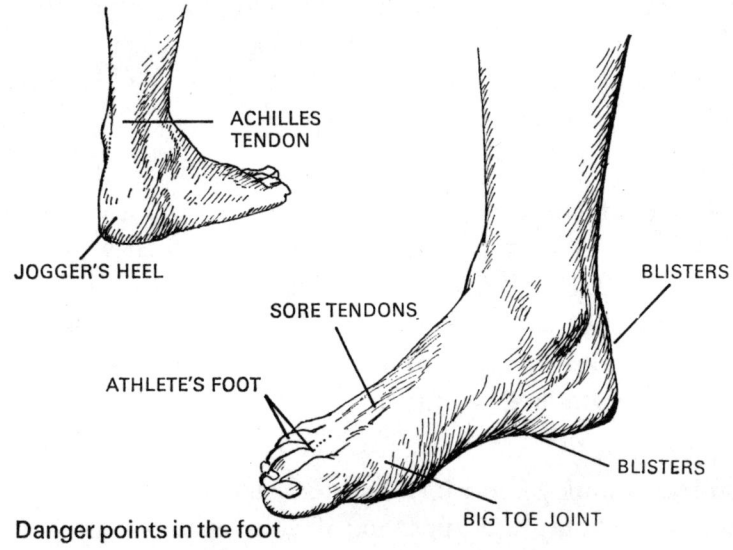

ACHILLES
TENDON

JOGGER'S HEEL

SORE TENDONS

BLISTERS

ATHLETE'S FOOT

BLISTERS

Danger points in the foot

BIG TOE JOINT

fungicidal cream or powder, and the treatment should be continued for two or three weeks after the signs have disappeared. Regular laundering of socks and towels will help to prevent it spreading.

Blisters and callouses

These are caused by shoes which do not fit properly, but if your socks are not clean they too may cause friction. Some people have very tender skins, and may get blisters by running only a couple of miles. They need to take special precautions. Canvas shoes are worse for blisters than proper soft leather running shoes.

I do *not* recommend putting on surgical spirit or anything else to harden the outer skin – this often leads to a deeper and more serious blister. Two devices used by marathon runners are: putting a thin coating of vaseline on the sole of the foot before putting socks on, or wearing thin nylon socks inside the woollen or cotton pair. When your shoes and socks are on, the shoes should not feel tight anywhere, but your feet should not be able to slide about at all.

If you do get a blister, treat it as soon as possible, by piercing it with a clean, sterilized needle and draining the fluid away. Do not remove the dead skin, but you may cover it with a plaster if it is going to be rubbed again. If you have good shoes, they will allow the sweat to evaporate, so that you don't get the rubbing of a sweat-soaked sock.

Sore tendons

You may get inflammation of the tendons running into the toes over the front of your foot. This happens particularly if your shoes are too big or if you are running on soft sand, because your toes have to work extra hard. The cure is to stop jogging for a few days and walk around in hard-soled shoes or boots that allow your toes to flex very little.

Sore big toe joint

If you start running too much and too quickly, you may get stiffness in your big toe joint, and if you carry on, the joint itself will become swollen and sore – what doctors call a traumatic arthritis. The secret is to take stiffness as a sign that you should rest, or at least jog very slowly. The cure is the same as for the sore tendons, and in both cases you should give yourself a week off jogging to allow the trouble to clear up.

Strained arches

If you have flat feet (fallen arches) you may get pain when you start jogging, because weight is being put on to joints in the middle of your foot which are not used to it. Again, a good pair of shoes with support under the arches, will prevent this. If you start with the beginner's programme, which has a lot of walking in it, your feet should gradually become accustomed to load-bearing. However, if you do get this trouble, the answer is to go back to shoes or boots which support your foot properly, and to walk regularly in these until the muscles have adjusted to the extra work. You can then go back to jogging – in the right shoes.

March fractures

These are so-called because they occurred in army recruits who were not used to marching. They are stress fractures of the bones in the balls of the feet, which become tender and then painful. The only treatment is to stop jogging, wear shoes which cushion your feet, and not to start jogging again until the tenderness has gone. Give yourself a week of walking before you start running and avoid hard bumpy ground.

Jogger's heel

Apart from blisters this may involve bruising or soreness in the heel itself, or inflammation at the base of your Achilles tendon. The latter is caused by shoes which fit too tightly around the heel, and can be cured either by stretching the shoe or by cutting away part of the rim of the shoe, or the pull-on tab.

Pain in the heel itself can be avoided by having a shoe which has plenty of cushion in it. It should have a rounded heel, so

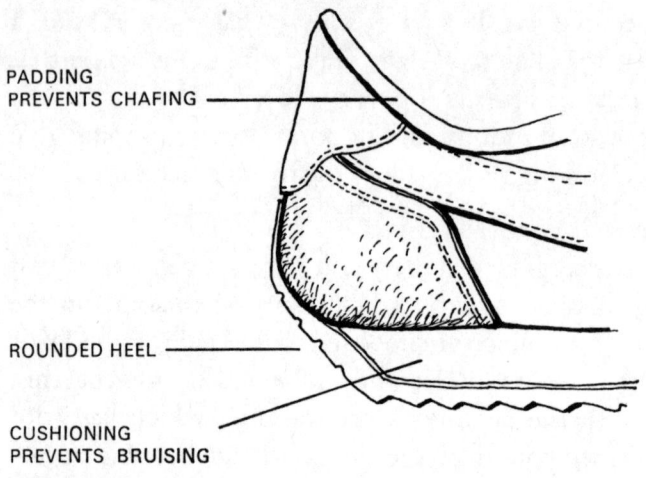

PADDING PREVENTS CHAFING

ROUNDED HEEL

CUSHIONING PREVENTS BRUISING

Heel of shoe in section

that your heel rolls easily as it strikes the ground. The cushioning may be built in like a wedge heel, or may be a separate heel cushion which can be inserted when it is needed.

The treatment for sore heels is to avoid hard roads, or to stop jogging altogether, and to wear shoes with a rigid, built-up heel for walking in. This will transfer the weight more on to the ball of the foot.

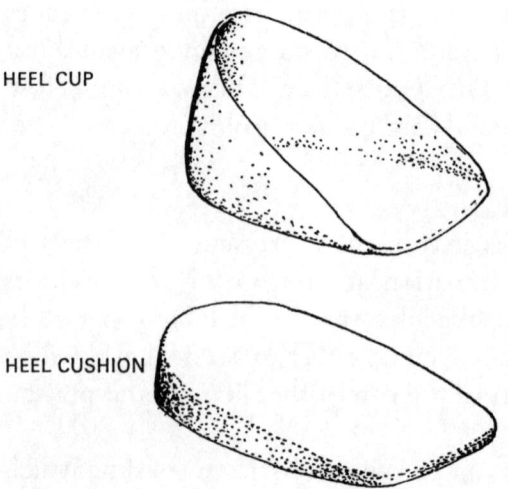

HEEL CUP

HEEL CUSHION

Detachable heel cushion and heel cup for the shoe

There is a tendency for the enthusiastic person who has a foot injury to go on jogging, adapting his foot action so that the pain is lessened. The result of this is that undue strain is then put on some other part of the foot, and a whole sequence of injuries may result. These are often more serious than the original trouble which could have been put right with a few days rest. So be warned!

Jogger's ankle
Included in this term may be strains on the inside or outside of the ankle, sprained ankles, or trouble with the Achilles tendon.

Strains
You get pain in the tendons on the side of your ankle from running on very soft or uneven ground, or from running along one side of the road on an uneven camber, so that one ankle is constantly at an angle. In either case the cure is to jog on firm level ground until the pain goes away.

Sprained ankle
If you put your foot into a hole, or stumble down a slope, you may turn the ankle right over, wrenching several tendons and ligaments. The ankle becomes swollen, stiff and painful on the affected side, and a bruise may occur. The immediate treatment of an ankle sprain is ICE therapy:

I – Ice (or cold spray)
C – Compression, with a bandage
E – Elevation: put your ankle up and rest it

The ankle should be kept as cold as possible and rested for 24 hours. After that you may go back to walking, keeping it strapped, but use discomfort as the guide and don't do anything that causes pain. With a gradual increase in walking, you should be able to jog again in a week, but stick to firm level ground, because the ligaments will take three or four weeks to recover fully.

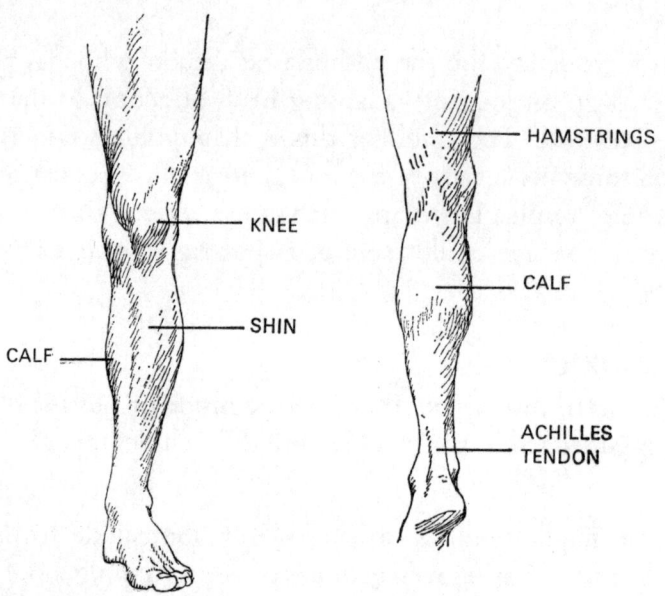

Danger points in the leg

Achilles tendinitis

This is one of the most common running injuries. The tendon becomes stiff, swollen, inflamed and painful, due to over-stretching. In extreme cases, where somebody tries to run fast on a stiff Achilles, the tendon may snap, needing surgical repair, so don't take unnecessary risks.

Achilles tendon trouble is brought on by running too fast, running too much on hard surfaces, and by not having enough heel support. It is one of the many troubles that come from not having good shoes. As soon as you start to feel any pain take a day off. The next day, make sure you have proper heel support, and jog slowly on level grass. If you can jog for two miles without any pain at the time or afterwards, you can go back to your normal schedule the next time out. I had a lot of this trouble when I was running across the USA and I cured it by walking in boots that had a firm built-up heel.

Jogger's leg

In this term we include both simple things like stiff calf muscles and more serious complaints due to stress fractures.

Muscle stiffness

This is just due to fatigue in muscles which are not used to prolonged work. Your calf muscles will get stiff if you are running up hills, and if you are running on your toes too much. The treatment is rest, soaking in a hot bath, and walking instead of jogging until you are no longer stiff.

Use of liniment or a cream such as Deep Heat will help to dissipate slight stiffness at the beginning of a run; but if the stiffness is slight it will go after five minutes anyway.

Use of loosening and stretching exercises before and after running will also help prevent stiffness, but the rule should be *not* to run on stiff muscles – it can lead to torn muscles. A muscle tear or pull should be given the ICE treatment (see page 117).

Shin soreness

This may start off just as stiffness down the front of the legs, which becomes more and more painful. It is caused by running on hard ground, running downhill, running too fast and running in shoes which do not have enough cushioning. Treat it as for stiffness – rest, soaking, and a gentle rub – and do not start again until it has cleared up. Beware of running on the road too much – this is the main cause of shin soreness. Prolonged shin soreness is often followed by a stress fracture.

Stress fractures

These are caused by too much running on hard ground, and they will not arise if you pay attention to the previous two sections. The symptoms are an ache in the front of the leg, either above the ankle or below the knee, which occurs during and after jogging, and gradually becomes worse as the days go by. The treatment is, firstly, to have an X-ray to find out where the fracture is, and then to rest for several weeks. In extreme cases the leg may have to be put into a plaster cast to protect it. This will only happen if you are unwise enough to go on running when your legs are already tired and stiff.

Jogger's knee

Knees, like ankles, are complicated things, and can be upset by twists, knocks and over-use. In the early stages of jogging your knees may not be able to stand the unaccustomed strain of your body weight bouncing up and down on them. This is why it is a good thing to walk before you run, because the muscles around the knees will get stronger and give more support.

Wrenched knee
This is similar to a sprained ankle and should be given the ICE treatment.

Torn knee cartilage
This may happen as a result of a bad wrench, and if the knee tends to 'lock' or give way after recovering from the sprain, see your doctor.

Pain around the kneecap
This may happen if something, such as an old piece of scar tissue, interferes with the smooth movement of the flexing of the knee. The immediate treatment is rest, followed by walking. If it persists, see your doctor – there are various ways of getting rid of the offending fragment. It may simply be due to over-use of a tendon, in which case rest will cure it.

Fluid on the knee
This is generally caused by a hard knock. The knee should be rested, and if the swelling does not go down after a day, see a doctor.

Bursitis
Bursae are small sacs of fluid which occur in various parts of the body, between tendons and bone surfaces. There are several of these around the knee joint which, when inflamed, swell up and cause pain. The best known are 'house-maid's knee' on the front of the kneecap and 'clergyman's knee' immediately below the kneecap. As the names imply, they are

caused by too much pressure on those regions, and should clear up with a few days' rest – if not, see a doctor.

Cartilage operations
Many rugby players, and other sportsmen, have cartilages removed at some time in their career. Should they jog? Yes, they should. As long as they pursue a sensible programme, their knees are likely to give less trouble than if they were to become totally inactive. They should be more careful than most about running on roads and uneven ground, because they have less protection within the knee joint.

Jogger's thigh

The only troubles joggers are likely to have with their thigh muscles are due to fatigue. Stiffness of the hamstring muscles is caused by trying to run too fast, sprinting or running up hills. What I have already said about stiffness in the section on jogger's legs applies here.

If you go on a really long run, on a sponsored jog, for instance, you may get stiffness in the muscles at the front of your thighs, just above the knees. The cure for this is plenty of rest.

This raises the question of how long a run you can manage on occasions like this. The human body has a great ability to manage a one-off effort – sometimes people who have done no training can go out and do a 30-mile sponsored walk or jog. The real test, however, is what their condition is on the following day.

As a rule of thumb, on a single occasion you can cope comfortably with a distance which is $2\frac{1}{2}$ times your daily milage. If your regular jogging distance is 3 miles in 24 minutes, you will be able to manage 7 or 8 miles if you really have to. They will not be done as fast, of course. Your average speed would probably be about 10 or 11 minutes per mile in that case.

If you are running on uneven stony ground, you may get stiffness or strain in the groin muscles, on the insides of your thighs. This will clear up in a few days if you stick to firm, level ground for the next few sessions.

Jogger's hip

This may refer to pain in the hip joint itself, or to strains in the muscles around the hip. The joint may become inflamed because it is not accustomed to such continuous use. A couple of days' rest, followed by a gradual re-starting of the programme, may solve the problem. Sometimes, however, the pain in the hip is a referred pain from the spine or the lower back, and the trouble may lie there – see the section on back trouble in Chapter 7.

Try running with a slightly different body posture: the trouble may arise just because you are too set in one position. Another thing which may bring improvement is doing exercises, such as sit-ups, to strengthen your back and ·stomach muscles. Try altering your stride length slightly while jogging, a few inches longer per stride, and then a few inches shorter, until you find the stride length which requires the least effort and causes the least strain. Many people run with too long a stride – you will notice how marathon runners pitter-patter along with a very short stride.

If the muscles around your hip joint and in your backside are stiff after your first few sessions of jogging, don't be surprised, just take the programme steadily and use the stiffness as a guide. If you are stiff after every session you are undoubtedly doing too much. Try reducing the length of the run by a third. It is much better to start by jogging a short distance regularly than to try to run a long way and have to take a week to recover.

Finally, remember that muscles work best when they are warm. Keep your track suit or tights on when the weather is cold, and put your gear on again as soon as you have finished training. Before a fast run, warm up for five minutes as described in Chapter 3.

Cramp

The most common place to get an attack of cramp is on the calf muscles, but you may get it in the foot or the thigh. It happens when you are overtired, and affects you most when you are unused to regular running. Experienced runners get it only after a very long or very hard run. It happens particularly when you have lost a lot of salt, by sweating, so be sure to keep up your salt intake as well as your liquids when running in hot weather.

The immediate treatment is to get hold of your leg and gradually stretch it in the opposite direction to the muscular contraction. This may sound painful, but it works well. If the cramp is in your calf muscle or the arch of your foot, get hold of your big toe and pull it upwards, straightening the leg out.

After the attack has passed, a bit of gentle rubbing will help you get over the discomfort. It is a sign that you have done enough for that day, but as long as you keep up your salt intake, the cramp alone will not affect you the next day, though stiffness may do.

10 Food for joggers

The guiding principle

In general health, the principle for eating is equilibrium. If you can balance the food you take in with the food you burn up, you will stay the same weight. If you replace the minerals and vitamins your body needs, as they are used up, then your body will be able to go on repairing and rebuilding itself, but if you don't then you may suffer from the ensuing deficiency. Very likely any ailments will never become so severe as to take you to the doctor, but mild forms of deficiency may make you more susceptible to infections, lacking in energy, slower to recover from illnesses or injuries. The jogger, being more aware of his body, is more likely to notice these effects in the early stages.

Trusting your instincts

This may make sense when you are a child, because the child's body is capable of burning up excess food. Even then instinct may be at fault, because man has a sweet tooth. In former times this may have helped him to seek out quick energy foods like wild honey, but in these days of plenty the sweet tooth is a menace to health, leading to bad teeth and the consumption of a lot more calories than we need. When we get older, and the age varies a lot from person to person, we lose our ability to burn up the surplus, and so it just accumulates in the form of fat. From 30 years of age onwards we have to think about what we eat.

The ins and outs of eating

You need a basic amount of food to keep you alive – to keep your heart beating, your liver working and your lungs breathing. This uses up a lot of calories – between 1500 and 2000 calories a day for the average person. Again, individual differences are considerable. Some cases were discovered recently of women who put on weight on a diet of only 1000 calories a day – which most experts would have considered impossible. People of the same weight may burn up very different amounts of food per day, depending on what is called their Basic Metabolic Rate. The thin, hollow-cheeked characters you see around very probably owe their thinness to inheritance rather than exercise. The unlucky ones with a low BMR put on weight very easily.

However, when you start to take exercise, life is much fairer. The more energetic the exercise, the more calories per minute you will burn up. Moreover, the bigger people, who have more weight to carry about, will burn up energy more quickly through exercise than small people. An average person of 10 stones (140 lb) will burn up 100 calories per mile jogged, while a 14-stone (196 lb) man will be burning 135 calories per

FAT JOGGER   LEAN JOGGER

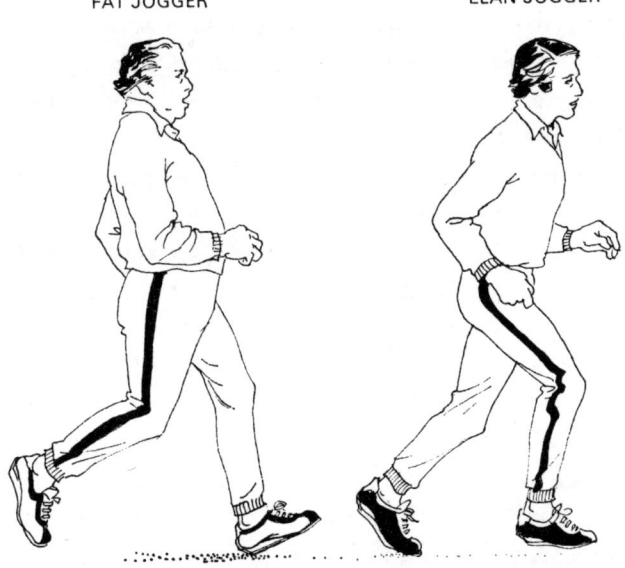

Excess weight makes running harder, putting an extra strain on the heart as well as upsetting the balance of the body.

mile. Funnily enough, the speed at which you jog has much less effect on the rate calories are used up *per mile*. If you compare it with the petrol consumption of a car, the heavy car will obviously use up more per mile than the light car. If you are going at maximum speed, your consumption will go up a little bit, say 10 per cent, and similarly it may drop 10 per cent if you are really crawling along. Of course, if you run fast you will use up more calories per hour. The 10-stone man, running at 8 minutes a mile, will do 7½ miles in an hour, using up 750 calories. If he runs 9 miles in the hour he will use up about 990 calories, and if he does only 6 miles he will use up 540 calories.

How can we deduce from this our weight loss? Strictly speaking, going on the energy released when fat is broken down, a pound of fat is worth 3500 calories or about 30 miles. But when we take into account the heating factor and the stimulation of the resting metabolism I think that a fairer figure is a pound for every 20 miles. Therefore, if you are following my schedules and doing 10 miles a week, you can expect one pound of permanent weight loss every two weeks. This does not sound very much, but if you can keep it going for three months you will lose half a stone, besides the other improvements I have mentioned.

There must be a limit to the amount you can lose. When I was running across the USA I was doing 40 to 50 miles every day, and I should therefore have lost over two pounds a day. The reason that I did not – I only lost five pounds over the whole trip – was that I was eating a lot more, about 6000 calories a day.

How can you tell whether you are hungry or just being greedy? The answer is not to increase your eating at all when you start jogging. As you lose weight, the thickness of the fat layer under your skin will get less. You will get an altogether leaner and fitter look. When you are *lean* and hungry, not just hungry, then you can afford to increase your food intake.

When to eat

If you accept the fact that, like most people, you probably eat too much, you must arrange things so that your opportunities for over-eating are as few as possible. You don't do this by skipping meals. If you do miss meals, so that there is a long gap between eating, your blood sugar is likely to get low, and you will feel lethargic and irritable. You are quite likely to go out and eat a doughnut or some other high-calorie food with no other nutritional value.

If you plan your day so that you eat small regular meals, with the right things in them, then you will maintain that vital equilibrium. It is essential that you eat breakfast, otherwise you may be going as much as 18 hours without food. The breakfast need not be large, and as most of us are in a hurry in the morning it is not too difficult to keep it small.

If you do your jogging in the lunch hour or when you get back from work, this too is going to cut down your opportunities for eating. The lunch hour jog reduces the time available and decreases your appetite too, in my experience. If you jog in the evening you are likely to miss out either on your cup of tea, or your glass of beer, or both. A lot of the time we are only eating and drinking for social reasons, and if you put the jog in place of the drink you probably won't miss it anyway. When the run is over you can enjoy the drink all the more in the knowledge that you are replacing what you have just lost.

Having had your after-work run, you will tend, therefore, to eat a little later: you will not be tempted to make yourself that extra sandwich before you go to bed. If you can keep to the routine of eating three times a day, allowing yourself drinks in between, but not snacks, then you are giving yourself a good chance of getting the situation under control.

What I have just said is directly opposed to the behaviour you will notice in serious runners, who are likely to eat three large meals a day, plus coffee and biscuits, tea and cake, extra fruit after meals and bars of chocolate in between. And they do it without putting on an ounce. The answer is that these people are not just jogging. They are running 10 miles most days of the week, and so using up an extra 6000 calories a week. Moreover, they have gone past the point, if it ever existed, of using up their fat reserves, because they have none, so they must replace those 6000 calories a week.

If you go running, there will come a point when you don't need to worry about over-eating at all, but you need to have run at least 2000 miles before you reach that point. The great thing about running is that it does allow you to eat, and you enjoy your food more.

What to eat

If you are going to take jogging seriously, then you ought to know something about what food does for you. There is a general feeling that some foods do you good and others are bad for you.

First of all, food provides you with energy, measured in calories or joules. Most of our energy comes from starch, sugar and fats. Some runners take glucose before a very long run because this is the quickest way of getting energy into the blood-stream. However, our natural stores of energy provide enough for well over an hour of intensive effort, so the jogger need not worry, unless perhaps it has been an energetic day and a meal has been missed. Given time, the body will use its stored fat as a source of energy, bringing about the weight loss I discussed in the last section. Starchy and sugary foods, and even fatty foods are therefore good for you up to a certain point, in that they give you the energy you need. The danger comes from eating too much of them.

The materials we need for growth and for replacing broken-down muscle tissue comes from protein, either animal protein, such as meat, fish, eggs and cheese, or vegetable protein in nuts, cereals and seeds of all kinds. We don't actually need very much protein, 100 grams a day, less than four ounces, is ample. It doesn't have to be animal protein, but animal protein does contain the ingredients we need in balanced amounts. There are highly successful runners who are vegetarians and the idea of steaks being necessary for runners is now completely outmoded. Eating too much meat is just as bad for you, maybe worse than eating too much starch, because it contains animal fats, which are associated with heart disease. Again, meat is good for you up to a certain limit, and bad for you in large amounts.

The body also needs minerals in small amounts. Iron is the most well known, because it is needed for the haemoglobin in the blood. If you are low in haemoglobin you become anaemic, and unable to run as fast. You also need calcium, sodium, potassium, phosphate, chloride, sulphate, fluoride and several others in very small amounts. It would be quite impossible to measure the exact amounts you need or the amounts which you get in your daily food. So long as you are getting a varied diet your body will select those minerals it needs and let the rest pass out. Minerals are not destroyed by processing, so that is one less worry. Spinach is said to be good for you because it contains iron, but so do a lot of other green vegetables. Milk is good for children because it contains calcium for bone growth.

Vitamins are controversial things. The only way of defining a vitamin is to say it is something that is essential in small quantities for survival. Fresh fruit, fresh vegetables, dairy foods, meat, particularly liver, eggs, and seeds, all contain vitamins. More and more are being discovered: does this mean we should go on taking more and more vitamin pills? No, it does not. Man has lived for hundreds of thousands of years without vitamin pills, and people in different parts of the world live, and run, on widely different diets. It does mean that your diet should have a lot of raw food in it, because many vitamins are destroyed by heating and by processing and storage. There is a danger in winter time, or whenever fresh fruit and vegetables become expensive, that you might be missing out on your vitamins. There is a simple solution to this. In the winter, put yourself on to a month's course of multi-vitamin pills. If you have been lacking in something, you should start getting the benefits of the vitamins by the second week, and you should notice an improvement in your general health and jogging performance for that month compared to the previous month. If you don't get any such improvement, you have proved to yourself that you were not lacking in vitamins.

Most vitamins are not stored by your body, so taking more than you need won't help at all. Taking twice as many vitamins as you need won't make you twice as healthy – it is just a waste of money.

Some foods are said to be good for you because they contain roughage. This is a vegetable fibre, which gives your intestines something to work on, and so helps to keep the food moving through your digestive system. If you are eating plenty of raw fruit and vegetables you will be getting all the roughage you need. If you are lacking in roughage, sprinkle bran on your breakfast cereal, and eat more wholemeal bread.

To sum up, the foods which are good for you, apart from foods which provide energy, are those containing high amounts of vitamins, minerals, proteins and roughage. But eating too much of them is likely to be harmful. However, you can hardly eat too much fruit and salad, because they are mostly water anyway, and contain very little in the way of calories.

Foods which are bad for you are the energy foods which are low in vitamins and minerals. They are alright for providing the extra energy but lack other things you need.

I really have not much sympathy with the health food fanatics. The additives and preservatives in our food are carefully monitored, and their main value is in stopping the food from going bad. As long as food is good to eat and contains the necessary food materials, it doesn't matter whether it has been grown organically or with the help of artificial fertilisers. The only harm you might encounter is the pesticide on the skin of vegetables, so you should thoroughly wash or peel raw foods.

We take a lot of trouble with our food at home, in order to enjoy it. Eating is one of the great pleasures of life, and if you run a lot of you can eat well. Fresh foods have the most flavour, so we grow some of our own fruit and vegetables. We pick wild mushrooms and blackberries, we get fresh fish, prawns and crabs at the seaside, we try to find the best supplier of meat, butter, cheese and eggs, and the best baker for bread. That, I feel, is time much better spent than that given to fretting over calorie counters and vitamin charts.

A few fallacies

'Sugar and white bread are bad for you.' Neither sugar nor white bread contains substances which are actually harmful. A few people suffer from allergies to wheat flour. *Too much* of either is bad for you, because sugar in particular contains nothing but calories. Most of the athletes I know take sugar on their cereals and in their drinks – it is a cheap and quick way of replacing the energy used up in running.

'Butter is bad for you.' 'Fried foods are bad for you.' 'Eggs are bad for you.' 'They all contain cholesterol.' Cholesterol is a substance which the body needs in small amounts. If you eat too much carbohydrate (starch and sugar) *and* you are eating a lot of fatty foods *and* you are eating a lot of eggs, *and* you are taking very little exercise, then there will be an accumulation of fats in the body, and the cholesterol count will increase, and the arteries will harden, leading to a greater chance of high blood pressure and heart disease. However, if you are eating normal amounts of food, without too much carbohydrate, you need a certain amount of animal fats, so the butter will do you no harm at all; nor will the eggs or the fried food. Moderation is the answer – and jogging, of course.

If you look back to my remarks about fats in the blood-stream in Chapter 1, you will see that running is the best possible antidote to the damaging effects of animal fats on the cardiovascular system.

Sample menus

It should be possible for you to construct your own sensible eating plan, based on what I have already written, but some people might prefer actual menus. The principle is really the avoidance of an excess of anything. Regular meals are best, but the body does its account on a weekly basis, and it is really by balancing miles run, food eaten, and weight gained or lost *over the week*, that you get a true picture of what is happening.

Jogging and slimming menu

This is low on calories, high in everything else. It should not be started until you have already become used to jogging on your normal diet.

Breakfast:	Fruit juice. Cereal with milk. Toast with butter but *no* marmalade. Tea or coffee with milk but no sugar.
Mid-Morning:	Coffee or tea, preferably without sugar.
Lunch:	Cheese, salad and wholemeal bread (with butter or margarine). Fresh fruit.
Mid-afternoon:	Tea, if you need it, without sugar.
Supper (after jogging):	Vegetable soup. Meat, fish or chicken, with vegetables. No bread. Fresh fruit or cheese. A glass of beer, wine or cider.

There is plenty of liquid in this menu, and it should be possible to get enough variety into the meat, cheese and salad dishes to prevent it from becoming boring.

Jogging menu

Breakfast:	Fruit juice. High-fibre cereal or porridge with milk and a little brown sugar. Toast, butter and marmalade. Tea or coffee, with milk and sugar if required.
Mid-morning:	Tea or coffee.
Lunch:	Wholemeal bread and butter. Cold meat or cheese with fresh salad. Fruit or cheese and biscuits. One drink.

Tea:	A cup of tea and a biscuit if you are eating late.
Supper:	Meat, fish, chicken or eggs, with potatoes, pasta or rice and green or yellow vegetables. Dessert or fresh fruit or cheese and biscuits. One drink before or with the meal. Tea or coffee afterwards.

The marathon diet

I mention this because anyone who is interested in running may hear it referred to. It is also known as the 'bleed-out' diet. The principle is that your body is deprived of sweet and starchy foods for three days and then, 48 hours before the race, it is given as much as it can take. To compensate for the previous starvation, the body stores up more energy than usual, in the form of glycogen, in the muscles and the liver. This means that in the marathon the body's carbohydrate fuel reserves, instead of running out after two hours as usual, will last for the $2\frac{1}{4}$–$2\frac{1}{2}$ hours needed for the race. Has this any application to the daily jogger? None at all. There is no magic food or diet which is suddenly going to make you fitter.

Eating and drinking on the run

Marathon runners do this, and there is some evidence that it helps in races or runs over 15 miles long. The food is taken as glucose, which is the most easily absorbed form. Both food and drink are taken in small quantities so as not to upset the stomach. If you are jogging only three or four miles you don't need anything – there is enough fuel in your body's reserve store. The only time when it might be necessary to drink is when you are running on a very hot day, if you go a little further than usual and start to get hot and dehydrated. It is possible to jog slowly immediately after eating and drinking, but you will soon become uncomfortable if you try to run hard.

Vitamin chart

Vitamin daily requirement	What it does	Sources
A 0.75 mg	maintains healthy skin and prevents eye trouble	butter, margarine, milk liver, spinach, carrots
B_1 1.2 mg (Thiamin)	necessary for obtaining energy from food	bread, flour, meat, milk, eggs, vegetables cereals
B_2 1.7 mg (Riboflavin)	as for B_1	milk, liver, meat, eggs, cereals, cheese, Marmite
B_3 1.8 mg (Niacin)	as for B_1; prevents pellagra	milk, bread, flour, meat, cereals
B_6 (Pyrodixine) rarely deficient	needed for protein metabolism	meat, fish, eggs, cereals, vegetables
B_{12} rarely deficient	assists in blood cell formation	liver, eggs, cheese, meat, milk
C 30 mg (Ascorbic acid)	growth of tissues and wound healing	potatoes, green vegetables, oranges, most fruits
D 0.0025 mg	needed to maintain calcium levels	margarine, fish, eggs butter
E rarely deficient	necessary for fertility	vegetables, oils, cereals, eggs
Folic acid rarely deficient	assists B_{12}	liver, raw green vegetables, beans, bread

Mineral chart

Mineral	Source	Daily intake	Needed for
Calcium	milk, cheese, bread, flour, hard water	1.1 g	bones and teeth
Phosphorus	milk, cheese, eggs, meat, bread	1.4 g	bones and teeth, energy release
Potassium	vegetables, meat, milk, fruit juices	3.3 g	osmotic balance, muscle and nerve activity
Sodium	table salt, bread, meat products	4.4 g	
Chlorine	table salt, bread, canned foods	5.2 g	
Magnesium	bread, potatoes, vegetables	0.34 g	cell enzymes, energy release
Iron	meat, bread, flour, potatoes, vegetables	16 mg	for making blood, and myoglobin in muscles

The daily intake is generally much greater than requirement, by a factor of 50–100 per cent. Problems arise only when the mineral cannot be absorbed by the body.

11 A final word: the competitive spirit

The jogger is competing only with himself or herself. It is a personal battle which each of us can win, and gaining that mastery over yourself can be one of the most satisfying things in your life. However, it may well be that when you get fit you start going for fun-runs and running with or against other runners of your age group. Here is where you will discover whether or not you are a competitor. It is much more sensible to run at your own speed and set your own targets, but competitors don't do the sensible thing. They hate to be beaten, and they will drive themselves far harder when running in a race than they ever do in training. Here is where you will have to be careful. Don't start racing unless you have at least eight weeks of progressive training behind you. If you do push yourself hard, expect to feel bad at the end of the run – every true competitor does – and don't expect to be back to normal the next day, because you will probably feel some after-effects.

Competition is great fun – I have been a competitor for 30 years and I still haven't got it out of my system – but it does make big demands, so be sure you are prepared for them, and take advice from some experienced person about how hard you should try to run the race. And the best of luck!

Bruce Tulloh

Appendices

Useful addresses

To find your nearest jogging group, contact:

The National Jogging Association, Secretary Tom McNab,
9 Corder Close, Westfields, St Albans, Herts.

Your regional sports council: contact them through council offices,
or through The Sports Council, 70 Brompton Road,
London EW3 1PY.

Your local health authority.

To find your nearest athletic club, contact:

Southern Counties AAA, 70 Brompton Road, London SW3 1EY.

Midland Counties AAA, Devonshire House, High Street, Deritend,
Birmingham B12 0LP.

Northern Counties AAA, Rooms 288–90, Corn Exchange Building,
Fennell Street, Manchester M4 3HF.

Welsh AAA, K. Griffiths, 7 Channel View, Marcross,
Llantwit Major, South Glamorgan.

Scottish AAA, E. Murray, 25 Bearsden Road, Glasgow G13 1XL.

To find details of Fun Runs, look in the publications listed below:

Athletics Weekly, 344 High Street, Rochester, Kent ME1 1DT.

Jogging, Stonehart Publications, 13 Golden Square, London W1.

Executive Health and Fitness, 3 Fleet Street, London EC4.

Conversion table

Weights

1lb	=	0.45 kg
5lb	=	2.26 kg
10lb	=	4.53 kg

Measures

10ft	=	3.04 metres
15ft	=	4.57 metres
100ft	=	30.48 metres

Distances

1 mile	=	1.6 km
5 miles	=	8.04 km
10 miles	=	16.09 km

Comfortable